THE EVOLUTION OF URBAN FORM
TYPOLOGY FOR PLANNERS AND ARCHITECTS

THE EVOLUTION OF URBAN FORM
TYPOLOGY FOR PLANNERS AND ARCHITECTS

BRENDA CASE SCHEER, AICP

Copyright © 2010 by the American Planning Association
205 N. Michigan Ave., Suite 1200, Chicago, IL 60601-5927
1530 15th St., NW, Suite 750 West, Washington, DC 20005-1503
www.planning.org/plannerspress

ISBN 978-1-932364-87-3 (hc)
978-1-932364-88-0 (pb)
Library of Congress Control Number: 2010912315

CONTENTS

LIST OF ILLUSTRATIONS

ACKNOWLEDGMENTS

I am grateful to Anne Vernez Moudon and Kiril Stanilov, who introduced me to the field of urban morphology and have acted as mentors, colleagues, and friends. Dr. Moudon also established and promoted the International Seminar on Urban Form (ISUF), an interdisciplinary and international group of scholars, which has nurtured me and others like me in our studies in this area. Within this group, I am particularly influenced by the work and conversations of Michael Conzen, Jeremy Whitehand, Jean Castex, Karl Kropf, Terry Slater, and the late Jacqueline Tatom. I believe that the founding fathers of the typo-morphology revival of the mid-to-late 20th century are yet to be mined for the complexity and immediate application of their remarkable ideas; they include M. R. G. Conzen, Gianfranco Caniggia, Salvatore Muratori, and Aldo Rossi. My contribution to exposing their work is a small tribute to them, and my hope is that a new generation of planners and designers will take a careful look at these giants.

I am grateful to the encouragement of my former colleagues at the University of Cincinnati School of Planning, particularly Charles Ellison, Nan Ellin (currently at the University of Utah), David Edelman, Michael Romanos, and the late Sam Noe.

Now in Salt Lake City, I have a found a home of terrifying beauty and incredible growth, creating an opportunity and an obligation to observe and act. Utah is inspirational on so many levels. At the University of Utah, where I am dean of the College of Architecture and Planning, my faculty and staff colleagues have resisted the temptation to tie me to the desk with administrative tasks and have welcomed my forays into teaching and writing. I am particularly indebted to Senior Vice President David Pershing, who has encouraged me in every way. Jenny Lind, Shaleane Gee, Peter Atherton, and Kathy Thompson have simplified my complex life.

This book is the result of many contributions and readings, most helpfully from my editor, Timothy Mennel, as well as Emily Talen, David Scheer, and Ken Bloom. My urban planning students patiently read the manuscript as part of their classes, and their insights were helpful in bringing clarity to the work.

This book would not have been possible without the hundreds of discussions and vetting of ideas that my architectural partner and husband, David Scheer, and I have had over the past 16 years. David is both inspiration and provocateur. I have to say that most of the original ideas in this book could be attributed to him as much as me. My two daughters, Casey Raim and Carrie Scheer, have tolerated and even admired their mother's "nerdiness" in ways that are both flattering and touching. Their support was essential for the peace of mind required to complete this. Finally, I could not have achieved what I have without the devotion and encouragement of my parents Calvin and Betty Case, who assured me I could become whatever I could dream.

THE EVOLUTION OF URBAN FORM

TYPOLOGY FOR PLANNERS AND ARCHITECTS

CHAPTER ONE | A CRISIS IN THE URBAN LANDSCAPE

We know how to design cities. Designers can whip out attractive watercolor drawings that envision a rejuvenation of our sad urban landscape of strip malls, car dealerships, fast food kiosks, ragged garden apartments, wide parking-dominated streets, and isolated subdivisions. If the new urbanism had not already offered us clear examples of better design, we have but to walk the streets of Paris or Savannah, Georgia, or St. Petersburg, Russia, to breathe in ancient and timeless lessons from our ancestors.

So why is it that for every much-heralded 50-acre new urbanism gesture, there are literally thousands of acres of new strip malls, gas stations, apartment complexes, office parks, subdivisions, and big box stores?[1] Multiscreen theaters, convention centers, soccer stadiums, airports, and shopping malls all resist the good urbanism lessons. Observe the far edge of any city: Why do big box stores proliferate like weeds in a garden, despite the efforts of planners and designers? What is it that we don't understand that confounds our attempts to change this ubiquitous landscape?

Planners and designers have been searching for the answers for some time, with mixed results. One probable culprit is ordinary land-use regulation, which can prohibit good urbanism.[2] There is considerable merit in this idea. Twentieth-century building has evolved in unanticipated ways, such that zoning has had a very limited effect on urban form. Zoning is not oriented around a formal plan; rather, a zoning map has blocks of color that describe the perimeters of a regulated area. Land-use and zoning plans indicate none of the apparatus that might constitute an urban design: street layouts and sizes, parcel size and shape, public space, building form, and scale. A land-use plan frustrates urban density and spatial form with its metrics of setbacks and floor area ratios that are driven by the goal to limit intensity and isolate uses. Parking ratios, subdivision regulations, and separation of uses can also prevent a well-designed urban form. A predominant opinion among planners and designers is that if we could change the regulation, we would produce more compact and livable cities.

A second prominent idea is that, as a culture, we have forgotten what is good and we need to be reminded through examples.[3] If only we could show people that dense urbanism is attractive and healthy and socially interesting, they would come to demand it everywhere. If only we could all develop a shared ideal about what is livable and good, as people who lived in traditional urban environments apparently did, we would be able to build it.

Both of these answers to the question of why we don't make cities the way we should—inadequate regulation or lack of appropriate examples—make a leap of faith: The proper, that is, traditional, urban form will blossom, eventually crowding out the strip mall and big box weeds if only regulation can be aligned and better design can be demonstrated to the public. It is assumed that in order to redesign our cities and suburbs according to smart growth principles, our culture will need to produce new building types on a grand scale. For example, big box stores should be replaced by mixed use types, and low-density single-family homes by higher-density types.

In this book, I offer a different perspective, born of research in many different places over time. In any one place, most buildings conform to one or another of a limited set of building types—for instance, a strip mall is an example of a type. These types are used over and over because they align with the conditions of the culture and economy. In other words, they emerge or evolve as a complete resolution of a complex, interwoven set of problems. As long as the conditions that gave rise to the type continue to exist, the type will proliferate, with minor variations. Only when conditions change will these types evolve to respond to the new conditions, with some allowance for natural resistance to change. Changing types on a grand scale so that they emerge naturally is difficult without first creating a corresponding change in these conditions. Thus it is that big box stores, for example, continue to be far more prolific than mixed use retail types.

Managing the dynamic of typological change is an essential skill for planners. Yet most urban design ideas are based on a static understanding of the built environment, and they anticipate an end, when the plan is complete. A master plan is an imagined future environment, a blueprint or framework to get from one point of time to a day in the future. Few plans actually are completed with any fidelity, however, for a variety of reasons. A major one is the simple fact that conditions of the urban economy and culture change too profoundly and too frequently for the master plan to be relevant for a long period of time. A plan that is a singular vision, or which is very precise, may not have the flexibility to be adapted for these changes. This is a confounding problem for planning in general, but especially for urban design, whose pretty pictures can seem laughable 20 years down the road. Like an old science fiction movie, planners' illustrated visions of the future can seem oddly anachronistic in ways that written documents might not.

This dilemma cannot be easily solved. Design, for designers, has historically meant the creation of an object. Urban design, as practiced, assumes the creation of an object, albeit a rather large and complicated one with multiple parts built at different times. Alternatively, many urban designers now understand urban design less as the creation of a series of specific buildings and open spaces and more as a framework for change that is continuous and ever evolving.

In plotting an urban design strategy, planners can manipulate or limit the conditions that affect and change the physical environment over long periods of time. This requires an understanding of the normal dynamic forces that operate on the built landscape. Some of these forces are obvious to planners: zoning, markets, transportation, and so on. What is not well understood is the mechanism by which these forces work their magic. Why does a big box store happen, or a strip mall? How can we change these places? Often the frustrating answer is that, despite our knowledge of better ideas, we cannot change them; instead, they keep popping up. These ordinary building types are persistent, ubiquitous, and resistant to the planner's bag of tricks.

Since ordinary building types are the most visible building blocks of the urban landscape, planners must study the naturalized conditions under which they arise, flourish, and change to have any hope of transforming them or the urban landscape that contains them. By understanding types as emergent from culture, we can recognize that it is not possible to invent new types or substantially alter a type solely for the purpose of serving a different kind of urban design idea; these attempts betray a fundamental misunderstanding of how the urban environment creates and recreates itself. Instead, we must see types for what they are: natural adaptations that satisfy a specific set of conditions. It is the conditions themselves that can be manipulated, not the type.

A wholesale change in the urban environment cannot be accomplished without orchestrating this evolution. This book is about understanding how types originate and evolve, so that planners and designers can help to manipulate this change effectively with the tools at hand. Assisting and encouraging the evolution of common types is, in the long run, the only way to ensure that more urban types will be successful on their own terms— that is, that good types will appear more or less spontaneously, without excessive regulation to force them to happen. Manipulation of types requires a sophisticated understanding of building types and their relationship to urban form and the conditions that drive them. Although we can imagine an ideal city, it may not be possible to build it or rebuild our urban landscape significantly unless the complicated processes of typological and urban transformation are understood.

That is not to say that altering the course of urban development is impossible in the long run. In less than a century, the urban and suburban form of the United States was dramatically reshaped by a combination of interrelated forces, including the globalization of the economy (which brought us Wal-Mart, for example); technological shifts in communication, construction, and transportation (cars, jets, electricity, TV, phones, steel, computers); the transformation of education, civil rights, and the role of women; the rise of corporations, governments; and so much more. The reason we do not build cities in the lovely traditional forms that we know from history is obvious: The patterns and types in older cities emerged from completely different cultural, technological, and economic conditions. The dramatic shifts over the past 100 years guaranteed that a new urban landscape would emerge to challenge the traditional form.

That emergent urban landscape is all around us, for better and worse. It reflects our shared values and embodies our expectations, which is why American cities are so similar everywhere. Citizens of older cities also shared similar common expectations of form, if not explicit values about how a city should be. Building types from the 18th and 19th centuries embody those expectations. In the same way, our contemporary building types, like it or not, also embody the habits, values, society, and economics that have lately evolved.

There are good reasons why designers are not satisfied with the types that emerge from cultural processes. Our shared values have serious problems and weaknesses that are worth questioning. Are Wal-Mart and strip shopping centers the best we can do? Are incessant growth and expansion necessary for quality of life? It is worthwhile and perhaps even critical to take on the complicated task of deeply understanding the emergent types that surround us and the conditions that create them. It may even be possible to push evolutionary change to happen more quickly by manipulating the conditions under which these types thrive.

Consumer values and expectations are components of these conditions. Seen in this way, the design and construction of an idealistic new urbanism project does not represent an evolutionary shift but a form of consumer advertising that may slightly influence the slow process of typological change over time.

At present there are many exemplary urban-style projects that are featured in design media. Most of these arise from very particular situations that almost always include massive control of a single large site. These exemplary projects can be seen as leaps, not evolutions. Most exemplary projects give preference to satisfying ideals: The formal and imagistic attributes of a place predominate. As a result, they must often overcome enormous resistance to be built at all. This resistance can take the form of irate neighbors, reluctant bankers, planning regulation, dicey market studies, parking needs, and a host of other cultural and economic barriers. Because they have not emerged or evolved from the crucible of complex cultural conditions, these exemplary projects cannot be expected to proliferate naturally. Although they may be financially successful—our ultimate measure of value in this culture—they are still much riskier than "normal" development.

This book undertakes the task of unraveling the idea of building types as emergent forms that drive most urban development and transformation. By studying types and how they change over time, designers and planners can become connoisseurs of the physical environment, easily recognizing a wide variety of urban patterns and able to classify, date, and analyze the strengths and weaknesses of them.

Building *type* is an idea that actually has many related but different meanings in architecture. Typologies are classification systems, with important uses in fields as different as linguistics and biology.[4] In architecture, the most common use of the term describes a loose classification of buildings based on their primary use—library, school, airport, for example. Buildings of the same use-type have the same function but may take many different configurations. Later in this chapter, I will describe use-types and other ideas of building types, but everywhere else in this book the word *type* will be used to describe formal types. Formal types share characteristics of the same form—for instance, a big box or a row house—but may be adapted easily for many different functions, even though they may be commonly associated with one function and originally derived from that function. Form types are particularly useful because they constitute a way of analyzing and describing the space, shape, density, and many other physical configurations of the built environment. Just as the term *land use* does not give us much information about the physical configuration of a place, use-types—library, retail, and so on—do not tell us the shape or scale or configuration of buildings.

Formal types, on the other hand, can be used to describe the shape, feel, scale, and configuration of the environment but without being specific about the precise architectural character, building use, or intensity of activities. This opens up an important arena for planners and planning regulation. By describing the existing and future city according to building types and their urban configurations, planners have a tool that is oriented toward creating specific physical configurations of the city rather than—or in addition to—the economic and intensity configuration, or what is known as *land use*. Using type as a basis for physical planning also implies a certain flexibility and possibility for change—of use, character, intensity, and so on—that is missing in most regulatory systems.

In particular, planners who are creating form-based codes or aesthetic zoning are already involved in a regulatory system that relies on a sophisticated understanding and coding of types. This book is specifically intended to help planners understand the subtleties of the idea and answer confounding questions about use-type and formal types, architectural guidelines, site plans, and form-based codes, and how type is related to the urban form. In the next chapter, I also introduce a brief history of the idea of *type*, which can provide a background to those who want to understand the development of typology and morphology (the study of urban form) as developed since the Enlightenment.

In this book, I will be demonstrating the following four theories of type, which are derived from the study of the evolution of six American cities and towns, including several suburban examples:[5]

1. Most buildings are exemplars of particular definable types. These types are not arbitrary but represent the resolution of forces impinging on the building industry and culture in general at the time they were built. Types are not autonomous, plucked from previous eras and imposed in a new place. At their origin, they participate in a culture, which means that they interact with the culture and all its conditions. A new or transformed type can be introduced successfully on a grand scale only when the conditions for its introduction are right.

1-1 | Brownstone row houses such as these in Bedford-Stuyvesant, New York City, are a clear example of a type. Note the variation in details of windows, bays, cornices, and finishes, while the type has similarity in scale, proportion, overall organization, and features such as the tall stoop.

2. Because types emerge and evolve rather than being wholly invented, improving the built environment implies an understanding of how the process of typological transformation occurs, especially through changing conditions such as market demand, technology, cultural values, infrastructure creation, and regulation.

3. Typological observation is an important urban analysis tool. Existing environments reveal their recent and even ancient history through a close reading of their origins, common types, and their transformation over time. Signs of transformation are particularly informative: The story told by the observable typological and morphological process adds an unusually concrete and yet subtle confirmation of the written history of a place and is an essential step in urban design.

4. Building types in and of themselves represent ideas that are carried forward in time. This signification and historical continuity imbue building types with a design value and power. Designers often deliberately impose some historic typological characteristics on a new building in order to endow it with some of the significance of a historic type. As a culture, we vaguely recognize types and have expectations about them, which can be reflected—with subtlety or with more overt quotation—by the architect.

FORMAL TYPES

What is a type? A type is a class of buildings having formal characteristics in common, usually as a result of having certain global functions in common. There are several defining characteristics of a type: circulation, overall shape and scale, entrance conditions, and situation on the site. Building types are abstract. Each individual building of a given type is an exemplar of that type,

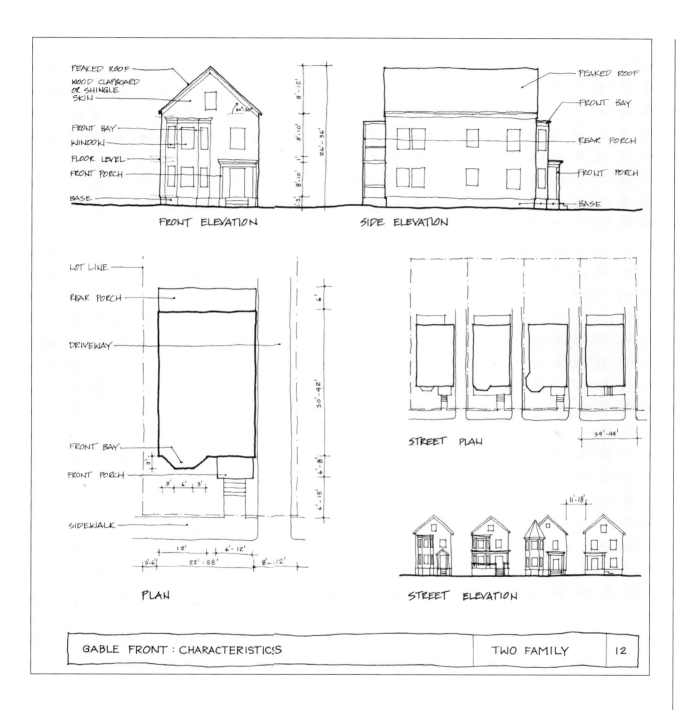

FRONT ELEVATION   SIDE ELEVATION

PLAN   STREET PLAN   STREET ELEVATION

| GABLE FRONT : CHARACTERISTICS | TWO FAMILY | 12 |

a variation that contains all the elements of the abstract term but may also look quite different from any other exemplar.

Take the example of a 19th-century row house: It has multiple stories; it is relatively narrow, with party walls; and it has small punched windows and a tall stoop (fig. 1-1). It is typically entered on one side of a three-part facade division, which indicates its internal circulation pattern. Stairs and corridors inside the building are along one side of the structure in a central

1-2 | Illustration from A Pattern Book of Boston Houses, *the summary of Boston's gable-front type that was used by the city in the 1980s to guide redevelopment. Note the nature of the characteristics that were called out.*

7

core, with front rooms and back rooms open to light. The row house was used primarily for residences initially, with an internal configuration leaving the main family with the first, second, and third floor; the uppermost floors were used by servants; and the lower level, beside or below the stoop, could be rented out.

As with most types, this type has a common site configuration relative to its neighbors and to the street. It is arranged in rows, usually lining the street, with a rear yard of varying depth. This type appears in many places and in many styles, with some variation in stories but not in proportion, original use, or site configuration.[6]

Each variation could be considered a different type, or for some purposes, within a family of similar types. There is not a systematic or universal nomenclature or classification of types; types are sometimes named and identified within regions—for example, Boston's triple-decker—but the same type could be classified or named differently in a different region (fig. 1-2). To complicate it even more, names like "row house" have no specific universal meaning.

Type is related to function but not precisely. We might consider building types to be the customary building of countless vernacular builders over time. The row house type just described is a common one in European urban culture because it fit very well with the conditions of its time. One of these conditions was the original use of the building, but a very precise fit with function is counterproductive to the useful life of a type. Buildings of a particular type may have significantly different functions as they exist over time. In the row house, the servants no longer live on the top floor, and the family may have long been replaced by a law office and four small apartments, all with minimal damage to the building or even to its fit with the original type abstraction. This flexibility of internal configuration, urban scale, and use, which is common in some types, gave the row house type a magnificent resilience. Over time, particular buildings may come and go, but the type itself can remain serviceable for many centuries by the means of minor transformations.

On the other hand, some types become obsolete more quickly, especially if they are tied inflexibly to a single function—for example, a blacksmith's shop. One of the most important forces of transformation is obsolescence. Types sometimes become obsolete or are regulated out of existence, a particular opportunity or concern for those who make policy.

In the United States, the flexible, attractive row house is in danger of such lethal regulation. The tall stoop of a residential row house is not accessible to people with physical disabilities. In most places, this means the row house can be built only as a single-family home, not as a place of business or multiple dwellings, which gives it its flexibility. With clever design, one can make a building that somewhat resembles the original, but not within the framework of the original type, which assumes that everyone will climb up and down. Even though historic row-house buildings continue to be popular—see Boston, San Francisco, Chicago, and Brooklyn, New

1-3 | *Newer-style town houses in Glens Falls, New York*

York—the type, with its inherent use flexibility, cannot be reproduced in a new neighborhood.

While we enjoy and still occupy older types such as row houses, their currency today is to represent a few ideas that we would like to retain, since it is difficult for row houses to satisfy contemporary conditions. We admire the urban environment, the public facade, the street character, the density, the scale, and the materials of the row-house type. But so far, contemporary adaptations of this type generally fall far short of the desirable 19th-century urban environment. The conditions under which a type arises are a cultural package, and it is difficult or impossible to separate out one or two desired characteristics of a row house without losing the integrity of the type altogether.

On the other hand, all types evolve. The row house has not directly evolved much in recent years in the United States because it has been edging toward obsolescence for many decades, even as a single-family home. It has no parking, it has a limited garden, its tall ceilings require expensive heating, and its height and vertical arrangement of spaces have fallen out of favor for residences. It must be built as a single-ownership unit with fireproof party walls. It is too narrow to adapt for large units that need width, light, and good circulation. To be occupied by more than one family or a business, it has to be equipped with an expensive elevator, further constraining width and light. These problems can be overcome in the Back Bay of Boston, or the Upper West Side of New York City, where property values allow these expensive adaptations, but for speculative building on a large scale, the row house of the 19th century can no longer be considered a model except as an image.

The great-grandchild of the row house type is the town house, a similar building in that it is built side by side in rows (fig. 1-3). The town house is a single-family building that may or may not have street frontage and rarely has a stoop. It may form a street wall or a courtyard with others. Its proportion

1-4 | Contemporary town houses in Austin, Texas, read as a single building ensemble, compared with older row houses. Note that the entry is level with the street, so privacy must be maintained with a wall.

and frontage are very different from the row house, because it lacks a stoop, each floor has a greatly diminished floor-to-ceiling height, and it usually has only three floors (though two floors are also common). In some forms, a garage constitutes the first floor, dramatically affecting the urban realm.

Just as important to the urban context and the public realm, the old-style row-house type was owned fee simple: It sits on its own plot of land and shares only a wall with its neighbor, not a contractual relationship. Built separately, one at a time, each row house was somewhat unique and sometimes had no architectural similarity to its neighbors except the loose characteristics of the type that they both exemplify. The owner customarily expected to extensively remodel both the outside and the inside at will, within a legal framework suited to continuous adaptability.[7]

The contemporary town house, on the other hand, is developed as part of an ensemble, a much larger project that has strong architectural similarity—scale, massing, detail, material, and landscape—and a much freer relationship to the site, parking, garden, and street. Even when owned separately, town houses are governed by private regulations, and it is difficult for an owner acting independently of the association that controls the complex to modify their own town house on the exterior or interior (fig. 1-4). This means that it is not nearly as flexible in responding to changes in cultural and social conditions. This particular constraint did not exist in the older row-house type.

Other definitions of type

This section will describe other uses of the word *type* so that we can understand how they are different from the formal type. A *use-type* is very commonly associated with architectural design. In this definition, a building type is a series of buildings that have an identifiable use, such as a library or recreation center. Architects study building types to assist with programming a new building, programming being the definition of spaces and their relationship, size, and requirements. Type studies primarily focus on unusual architecture, so standard configurations—say, a simple school plan with classrooms and a center hall—tend not to be documented unless they have significant innovations. Architects are interested in innovations, so looking at the latest library helps to visualize how the functional and stylistic characteristics of libraries are changing. Here is a listing of some non-residential use-types that are commonly studied:

The limitation of use-type in describing form can be illustrated by retail types. Formally, retail can function successfully in any of these types: an indoor mall, a lifestyle center, a main street, a strip mall, a freestanding store, a big box, and a drive-through. Retail uses can also be part of another dominant use, such as an airport, an office building, or a hospital. So designating a block of land as retail or commercial on a land-use or zoning plan tells us nothing about its eventual urban form. Similarly, knowing that a building is retail tells us nothing about its configuration.

Residential types commonly combine the idea of formal type and use-type. Residential types include row houses, lofts, garden apartments, courtyard houses, cottages, high-rise apartments, motels, and so on. While the characterization of use is key, all of these at least imply a certain formal arrangement, even if it is understood only vaguely.

On the other hand, there are other residential use-types that do not imply form at all: multifamily apartment, single-family house, dormitory, retirement home, monastery, shelter, or halfway house. Each of these can be designed with several different types.

Describing and showing examples of use-types helps architects to precisely program specific spaces: What are the common pieces and parts, and how do they work together? How big is a hotel dining room? Where is the kitchen in relation to it? Even more important are the technical conditions that are revealed in use-type study, such as laboratory configurations, the need for ventilation, the code requirements for exiting, and so on. These variables can be quite different and compelling in different uses. Expertise in these areas is valued and rewarded, and this is one reason why a use-type retains its power as an organizing idea for architectural practice.

Most of the time, there is no assumption of a standard formal arrangement or part in a use-type; in fact the innovative projects that appear in the architecture type study are singular and architecturally interesting buildings, not ones that demonstrate business as usual. The use-type is also inventive—that is, architects are encouraged to create new use-types through imaginative combinations of old uses or the recognition of new uses.

Architects, historians, and critics make extensive comparisons of use-types to analyze contemporary and historic modes of expression and to track and validate design trends. What does a cathedral of today look like? In a cathedral building type study, the critic might find several common themes of contemporary practice: soaring space and manipulation of light characterized

COMMON USE-TYPES*

Airport terminals

Art galleries and museums

City halls and other public buildings

Community centers

Courthouses

Exhibition and convention halls

Laboratories

Libraries

Hospitals and clinics

Monuments and memorials

Parking garages

Office buildings

Religious buildings

Restaurants

Retail buildings

School and academic buildings

Stadiums

Theaters

1-5 | *Ledoux's invention of new types was influential in the development of innovative architectural forms. This is the "house of the river guard," designed for Chaux, an ideal city.*

by streaks and patterns, deep shadows, and dramatic highlights. She might point out that today's cathedrals demonstrate a striking sublimation of iconography or even symbolism, that they are spaces scrubbed of overt religious expression and yet somehow spiritual and contemplative. There is no science in this interpretation: The examples chosen exemplify the themes because they were specifically chosen to do so, and those that did not were left out. Over time and with editing, critics can develop use-type comparisons to define iconography that has its own life, much as historians revisit or reinterpret the past to reveal patterns.

The pervasive confusion of formal type and use-type derives from historical patterns, where these ideas were much more difficult to separate. For example, a cathedral, in certain eras and regions, came in only one or two formal types.[8] The use and the form were very specifically aligned. Many use-types—schools, office buildings, factories—originated with this congruity of form and use, only to diverge as the culture, technology, and economy diversified.

Because designers enjoy the potential for invention that is glorified in the use-type, they also are compelled from time to time to invent new types. The *innovation-type* is an imaginary building created to propose an extraordinary idea that would propel the built world in a specific direction or toward specific goals, often idealistic in nature. Myriad examples of these exist, from Boullée and Ledoux (fig. 1-5), to Le Corbusier's Unité d'Habitation.[9] Innovation-types are like architectural experiments, speculative and not likely to emerge through the normal processes of typological evolution. They represent an idea that would be a special leap. Projects such as these are often heralded as new

1-6 | *Proposing a new type: Paul Lukez imagines complex buildings that span freeways.*

types, and they are interesting in their own rights as thoughtful reactions to specific contemporary conditions or as influential models for real buildings.

An innovation-type is a building intended to be used over and over, thus singular speculations cannot be classified as innovation-types. A project that speculates on using shipping containers for housing in many places and contexts is an innovation-type. Similarly, proposals for buildings over and under interstate highways, or thin buildings that line highways and mediate between pedestrian spaces and auto zones, are innovation-types in that they represent an idea about how to treat many such places that exist all over the world (fig. 1-6). These are speculative solutions that do not arise naturally, because they do not address most conditions of contemporary urban form: They satisfy only one or two conditions that are important to their inventor.

Innovation-types are rarely popularized or adopted in the way that their authors hope—as solutions—although some versions are built as examples, almost as experiments. Occasionally an innovation-type that is built will resonate very strongly and influence the evolution of similar forms.

Finally, a *prototype* is a building deliberately designed for no specific site and meant to be copied almost exactly, with minor adjustments in size and orientation to fit the conditions of different sites. Branded businesses—for

Innovation in architecture
↳ FORMAL TYPE /
USE-TYPE

13

1-7 | *Even a closed Taco Bell can be a logo for the brand.*

example, chain motels, McDonald's, and Jiffy Lube—all use prototypes, and so do some religious organizations and shoestring-budget public agencies such as school districts, fire departments, and transit authorities. Although based in economies of repetition, the prototype has other cultural conditions attached to it, especially its branding and marketing potential. A hallmark of prototypes often is that they are very easy to read; one might almost call them "logo" buildings. People are conditioned to interpret these buildings correctly and know almost instantly what experiences can be found inside. Even when they are vacated, they still have power: A Taco Bell prototype that has been stripped of its signage and abandoned for another use can still be easily associated with the brand (fig. 1-7).

ENDNOTES

1   Stephen M. Wheeler, "Built Landscapes in Metropolitan Regions," *Journal of Planning Education and Research* 27 (2008): 410.

2   D. Parolek, K. Parolek, and P. Crawford, *Form-Based Codes* (Hoboken, N.J.: John Wiley and Sons, 2008). This book is intended as a guide for planners producing form-based codes.

3   Witold Rybczynski, "Architects Must Listen to the Melody," *New York Times*, September 24, 1989. Like many critics of modernism, Rybczynski here argues that contemporary disorder is due to a lack of "collective wisdom" and "architectural good manners."

4   Lindsay J. Whaley, *Introduction to Typology: The Unity and Diversity of Language* (Thousand Oaks, Calif.: Sage, 1997). This book is a summary of the linguistic idea of type.

5   Brenda Scheer, "The Anatomy of Sprawl," *Places: A Forum of Environmental Design* 14, no. 2 (Fall 2001): 25–37; "Who Made This Big Mess?" *Urban Design*, Winter 2005, no. 93: 25-27; Brenda Scheer and Mintcho Petkov, "Edge City Morphology: A Comparison of Commercial Centers," *Journal of the American Planning Association* 64, no. 3 (Summer 1998): 298–310; and Brenda Scheer and Dan Ferdelman, "Destruction and Survival: The Story of Over-the-Rhine." *Urban Morphology* 5, no. 2 (2001): 15–27. These are research case studies of types and their urban patterns.

6   Eric Firley and Caroline Stahl, *The Urban Housing Handbook: Shaping the Fabric of Our Cities* (London: John Wiley and Sons, 2009). This book is an excellent and well-produced catalogue of high-density, low-scale urban types, both traditional and contemporary.

7   Anne Vernez Moudon, *Built for Change: Neighborhood Architecture in San Francisco* (Cambridge, Mass.: MIT Press, 1986). This is a groundbreaking study of a San Francisco neighborhood.

8   Sir Nikolaus Pevsner, *A History of Building Types* (London: Thames and Hudson, 1976). This is an iconic catalogue of use-types conflated with formal types in historical examples.

9   Anthony Vidler, "The Third Typology," *Oppositions* 7 (Winter 1976): 3–4; and *The Writing of the Walls: Architectural Theory in the Late Enlightenment* (Princeton, N.J.: Princeton Architectural Press, 1987). Vidler is a major force in the historic understanding of the idea of type, especially as it was understood in the Enlightenment.

Chapter 2 | The Origins and Theory of Type

To understand the origin of type is to understand the origin and legitimacy of architecture itself: Are types found in nature? Inspired by God? Evolved from some original primitive types? Or generated from rational principles? Even today, planners are referencing "ideal" building types as one way to judge whether a building conforms to the preferred type (making it more likely to be approved) or deviates from it (possibly leading to its rejection).

A simple system of classification is likely to have encoded the earliest buildings into "house" and "not-house." Since, formally, a house in a given culture is a simple form repeated over and over, *house type* conflates both form and use. Something that was "not-house" arose when cultures began to specialize functions: Priests and rulers needed temples, palaces, and storehouses. The differing forms of the temple type and the storehouse type reflected very different ideas about their relative place in the culture, especially their place in the cosmology.

Over time, the number of types and their variety became more sophisticated. Typology as a classification was not much remarked upon before the Enlightenment, since the differences in buildings were obvious and types were somewhat standardized within a culture. Before the Renaissance, architects passed along ideas of what a temple, a palace, or a basilica type should be, primarily by imitating or elaborating on previous examples. Occasionally architects would adapt a previous type for a new use. These types were sanctified and legitimized by imitation and by their presumed sacred origin. Scandal could ensue if "proper" models were abused.[1]

Houses were even simpler forms of imitation—copies of ideas that were so generally accepted over a given geographic area that the form was repeated without really considering any substantive alternative or variation, except through a very slow evolution.[2]

According to the architectural historian Anthony Vidler, in the 18th century Enlightenment theorists began proposing that legitimacy in architecture was not the result of divine approbation and that it might be otherwise created by nature or reason. The explicit understanding and classification of building types reflected a conscious effort to provide rational explanations for existing types and provided a rational legitimacy for architectural form.

2-1 | *Allegorical engraving of the Vitruvian primitive hut*

In particular, Enlightenment architects were interested in origins, as most Enlightenment thinkers were. To discover the first building and the succession of buildings that followed was to give architecture legitimacy not through God or imitation but through nature and the rational perfection of nature over time. The purpose of the search for origins was to legitimize certain formal ideas while declaring others to be degenerate. The approved ideas were known as *types*, using the word to mean abstract models.

Most of the initial rationales for origins included the imitation of nature, which the Abbé Laugiér proposed was man's first lesson in shelter. He embroidered on Vitruvius's primitive hut—a theoretical explanation for the first architecture that presumed tree trunks as uprights, with a roof of crossed branches (fig. 2-1). This hut, it was thought, might have provided man with all subsequent ideas of construction: tapered columns, peaked roofs, and details of joinery. Architecture evolving—being perfected—from this system would have columns with organic-themed capitals, for example. French Enlightenment theorist Quatremère de Quincy restated it this way: "One should turn one's eyes to the type of the hut in order to learn the reason for everything that may be permitted in architecture, to learn the use, intention, verisimilitude, suitability and utility of each thing."[3]

Types were at first defined as ideal models. This idea arose from the 18th-century admiration for Greek art and architecture, as opposed to the "degenerate" forms of the Baroque. Greek sculpture, for example, idealized the human body: No actual person was depicted in such an idealization, but instead the artist selected the perfect features, the perfect body, and so on.[4] Greek architecture, it was theorized, had been derived originally from the primitive hut and perfected over time through adaptation to human proportion, ideal climate, landscape, and freedom. The resulting architecture—for example, the Greek temple of the classical period—was seen as an ideal model for all architecture.

It was Quatremère, writing in the early 19th century, who for the first time used the word *type* in ways that are directly related to our understanding today.

> The word type presents less the image of thing to copy or imitate, than the idea of an element, which ought in itself to serve as a rule for the model. The model, as understood in the practice of an art, is an object that should be repeated as it is; the type, on the contrary, is an object with respect to which each artist can conceive works of art that may have no resemblance to each other. All is precise and given in the model, all is more or less vague in the type.[5]

Moving away from the historical practice of imitation as a legitimizing force in architecture, he defined building type as an ideal, abstract form of a building, not an actual example to be duplicated or closely imitated. With this distinction, Quatremère allowed the possibility that man (architects) could create new abstractions and forms (types), albeit he preferred that they did so within a system of ideals, which he believed could only be based on classical Greek architecture.

Quatremère was interested in origins as well, and he engaged the question, current at the time: Did ancient Greek architecture influence ancient Egyptian or the other way around?[6] Were there rational principles that drove their similarities? What could explain their differences? His thesis laid out the proposal that there were three forms of primitive building from which all architecture derived: the cave, the tent, and the carpentered building—that is, the primitive hut. Quatremère proposed that Egyptian and Greek architecture evolved from two different primitive types: the Egyptian from caves, and the Greek from carpentry. Any similarities were explained by slight cultural contamination. Furthermore, he speculated that Chinese architecture was evolved from tents, and the details and expressions of their design could be attributed to that. This idea specifically denied the sacredness of form and detail in favor of a rational idea of primitive man and his available resources and common living practices. Quatremère also believed that only Greek architecture had been fully developed and perfected, since it arose in perfect conditions of ideal climate and local materials, mature aesthetic and philosophic appreciation, and relative freedom of thought. This idea later influenced

2-2 | Durand's engravings of a number of basilicas at the same scale

17

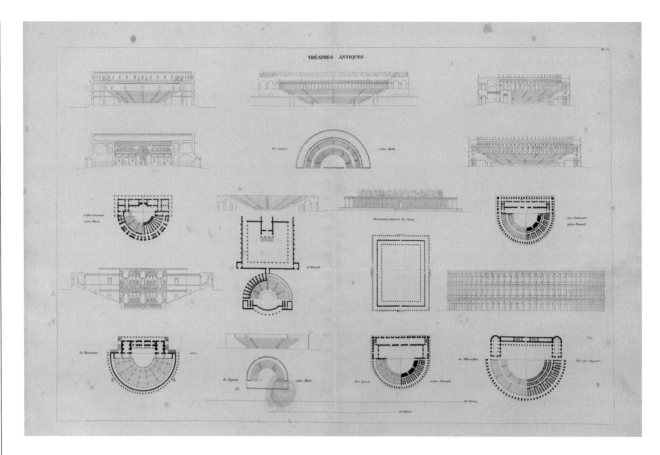

2-3 | Durand's engravings of different theaters at the same scale

those who believed that types were a resultant of specific conditions of place, history, and culture.[7]

At the same time that Quatremère was writing, J. N. L. Durand was a teacher at the École Polytechnique, one of the first formal training grounds for architects. Durand published two important books, which illustrated ideas of type in two ways. The first was his *Parallèle*, a huge, handsome book that reproduced plans, elevations, and sections of historic buildings at the same scale (figs. 2-2 and 2-3).[8] Used for generations by architecture students as a reference, it included examples from many traditions and cultures, not just classical. Importantly, Durand usually arranged the buildings in his *Parallèle* by functional and formal classification: churches, lodges, palaces, and so on. This reiterated the blossoming scientific idea of type: a classification system by form and function, inclusive of all important examples and without judgment as to their ideal nature.[9] By reproducing the buildings at the same scale and with the same drawing technique, Durand treated disparate examples as if they were scientific specimens.

Durand's second important contribution to the idea of type was quite different. As a teacher, he developed an ideal but rational system of architecture using columns, walls, and pure geometric forms, with the goal of allowing the architect to more clearly express the function of buildings without resorting to copying unsuitable classical buildings. Durand was particularly interested in rethinking function as a way of generating new forms, and creating architecture that could vary and yet have the legitimacy of working within a rational system of rules. These rules were derived from simple parts and simple geometry combined in specific relationships.[10]

In his book *Précis*, Durand proposed that using building systems in this manner freed the architect to discard imitation and address contemporary conditions through an infinitely variable system. His system required the architect to work with symmetry and classical elements, proportions, and materials, but it allowed the specific design to vary according to the needs of the building.[11] Durand thus invented a system flexible enough to accommodate the rapidly changing contemporary programs but restrictive enough to provide a uniform architectural standard (figs. 2-4 and 2-5).

Both Quatremère and Durand, although very different in their intentions, discarded mimesis as a legitimate force and completed the transformation of architecture from its basis in classical examples and divine inspiration to the rational justifications we know today. This rational basis for architecture would lead away from imitation and into the simple geometry that was assumed to be closer to original types, or geometric purity derived from ideal Greek form.

Durand, with his reliance on the generative qualities of geometry and rational functionalism, is considered one of the first modern architects, heralding a shift to legitimacy through rationality, a notion that persists today. Durand's system, a language of architecture, demonstrated the very powerful essence of building types: a way of designing that was neither entirely free of constraint nor overly prescribed, yet resulted in works that had automatic legitimacy.

In later generations, this generative principle gave the idea of type its power: Types are abstractions that follow certain rules (that is, contain certain widely accepted characteristics) yet allow the artistic interpretation of those characteristics, to the point where, as Quatremère wrote, "each artist can conceive works of art that may have no resemblance to each other."[12]

Some ideas thus produced in the Enlightenment include that type is a product of culture, that types provide a set of rules or characteristics but allow design variety, that types confer legitimacy as long as each type reflects specific kinds of values, and that types can support a rational classification system derived from both form and function. In the next period when the idea of type gained traction again—the middle of the 20th century—these ideas were transformed slightly and greatly expanded.

ROUND TWO: TYPE HAS A MOMENT IN THE SUN

Although the modern movement in architecture derived in part from the acceptance of typologies based on function and structure, modernists did not devote much discussion to the idea of type. Prototypes—that is, models intended for appropriation in different places—were common. For instance, Le Corbusier's Unité d'Habitation was intended to provide a model for high-rise housing blocks everywhere.[13] Repetition of industrial parts was one of the hallmarks of modernism, so modularity, modes of production, repetition, and universality of programs and forms overwhelmed subtle ideas about

2.4 | *Durand imagined a number of varieties of porches to be used in different conditions.*

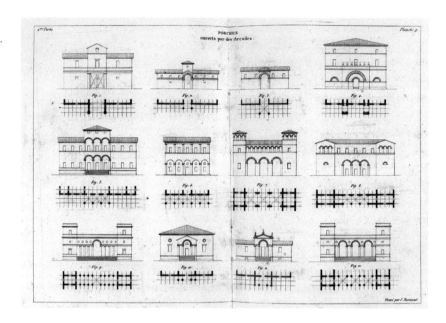

2-5 | *By drawing a variety of courtyards, Durand demonstrated for his students how the basic parts of columns and walls can be composed for variations in function and scale.*

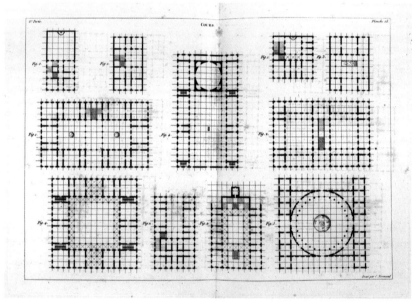

type, bringing modernism more in line with earlier ideas of mimesis rather than the more flexible notion of type.

Modernism's willful rejection of the extant city and desire to entirely remake the urban form led to a powerful reaction in the middle of the 20th century. Ideas of building type were revived as a way to recover and provide continuity with the fabric of old cities.[14] As these ideas progressed and changed in different intellectual settings, more or less vague ideas of typology gained great currency among architects and urban designers, peaking in the 1980s with the translation of a number of important treatises into English.[15]

The primary differences between the earliest Enlightenment ideas of type and those of the 20th century were the latter's emphasis on the city, and the role of building types in the city. In the Enlightenment, the city was not mentioned as a part of typological legitimacy or idealism, nor were the ordinary buildings of the city—the houses and shops—seen as worthy of consideration for architects. Types were recognized for public buildings, sacred buildings, and great palaces.

In the 20th century, this situation was reversed, with the ordinary fabric of the city becoming a revered model and the initiation of the "continuity of the city" ideal. Early in the century, modernists were focused on common structures such as mass housing, and these became an important arena for architects for the first time. But because modernist architects promoted high-density towers for cities, the separation of uses and transport, and the destruction of the crowded, infected old city, by midcentury the modernist project had many critics.

The Italians, in particular, mourned a crisis brought on by modern architecture's intent to destroy the historic urban fabric. They sought a design method that would act through the analysis of urban form to unite contemporary architecture with history and provide the urban continuity denied by modernism.[16]

In the 1950s, Salvatore Muratori and his disciple, Gianfranco Caniggia, helped to form the Italian school, which was a fertile group of architects who emphasized the nature of the crisis as a failure to understand or adapt to processes of change in architecture and the city (fig. 2-6). Through intensive study of Rome and Florence, they uncovered a rigorous method of discovering and defining types.[17]

Caniggia saw types not as reflective of an ideal but as organic, arising and changing according to specific conditions of time and place. The city was an agglomeration of these types, both the profane and magnificent, which varied over time and space. Any given urban type, he theorized, could be traced to a simpler type, an original type, and eventually all these types could be traced to a single-room structure. A particular type could vary in several ways: If it was in the middle of the block, it would likely be different than if it was on a corner, for example. Due to their slightly different traditions, a row house in Padua would have variations from a row house in Rome, even during the same historic era. Over time, the row-house type in Rome would itself evolve to be different than in earlier eras.[18]

Although this was primarily an analytical approach, most of the Italians were clear that their intentions were to appropriate these typological ideas into design. In a similar vein, the Krier brothers, Rob and Léon, abstracted ideas of geometric types found in the historic fabric—for example, a courtyard house—into generic forms and made suggestive transformations of these through formal manipulations (fig. 2-7). The results were a catalogue of types that recalled pieces of the city and that would fit with the city but did not relate to specific functions.[19] These were not meant to be inclusive, but suggestive of a method of design, in the same vein as Durand's *Précis*.

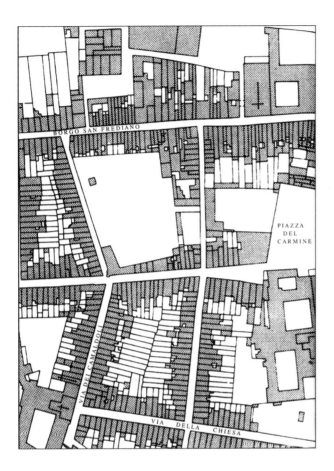

2-6 | Caniggia and Maffei compare two city tissues from neighborhoods in Florence in their analysis of urban form and type, from Interpreting Basic Building: Architectural Composition and Building Typology.

These Europeans viewed the typological project as a method of putting a stop to excessive individuality that was disruptive to the continuity of cities. They also saw it as a method of bringing contemporary architecture into alignment with the specific and unique nature of different cultures, which naturally had developed different urban forms and types over time. This was a specific critique of modernism, which deliberately internationalized and universalized architectural expression.

The most intensive and controversial message of the typological project, however, was the idea that types convey meaning. Architects can exploit these meanings in one of two ways: by using the type to relate specifically to a historical moment, as when a temple type is appropriated for use as a bank; or by using the type as part of a subversive or critical stance, as when a form associated with a prison is appropriated as a city hall. This technique, subtle as it is in using historic forms to convey critical themes such as the abuse of power, posed a real danger of being misunderstood, especially in the translation from Europe to the United States.[20]

Critics have suggested that the typological project reached its nadir when the critical stance was overcome by simple iconographic appropriation, which led to the postmodern historic pastiche so reviled by contemporary

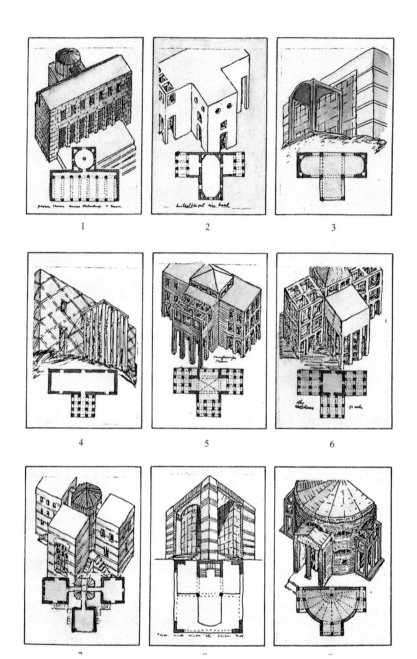

1

2

3

4

5

6

7

8

9

2-7 | Rob Krier's evocative drawing uses one diagram, of a two-story T-shaped type, to demonstrate architectural variations.

architects. Appropriation of historic motifs without the analytical and critical understanding of type and its relationship to the city was a degenerative situation that led to architecture that simply put a historic-looking face on a building without considering its urban situation or subtleties of type.[21]

The geographers of the English school approached the problem of the city far more analytically, and their discoveries informed others working in a more architectural vein. M. R. G. Conzen did not start out from a typological approach but discovered the importance of the town plan to the definition of a type.[22] Conzen proposed that the town plan—lots, blocks, and streets—was the underlying formal constraint of all buildings. In studying the city, he looked at both the ordinary situations of these configurations and also the unusual configurations that would present themselves—for example, in the "fringe belts" at the edge of urban development.[23]

Even after Italian and American architects exhausted the typological project as an overworked architectural moment, urbanists still continue to explore morphological patterns and their relationship to building types, developing an analytic approach that now encompasses cities of great variety on all continents. That approach is reflected in this book.

Although architects can be dismissive of the architectural misadventures of the late 20th-century typological project, new urbanists such as Léon Krier and Andrés Duany have significantly extended its urbanistic ideas, molding it into a populist movement that dismisses the excesses of modern architecture and the "elite" architects that work in that vein today.[24] It is due to this movement and its many supporters that ideas such as form-based codes and the legitimacy of type as a basis for judgment have become more commonplace.

ENDNOTES

1   Anthony Vidler, *The Writing of the Walls: Architectural Theory in the Late Enlightenment* (Princeton, N.J.: Princeton Architectural Press, 1987), 126.

2   Gianfranco Caniggia and Gian Luigi Maffei, *Interpreting Basic Building: Architectural Composition and Building Typology* (1979; Florence: Alinea Editrice, 2001), 43–45.

3   A. C. Quatremère de Quincy, "Type" [1825], introd. and trans. Anthony Vidler, *Oppositions* 8 (Spring 1977): 147–50.

4   Vidler, *The Writing of the Walls*, 125–38.

5   Quatremère de Quincy, "Type," 147–50.

6   Sylvia Lavin, *Quatremère de Quincy and the Invention of a Language of Modern Architecture* (Cambridge, Mass.: MIT Press, 1992), 42–61.

7   Ibid.

8   Jean-Nicolas-Louis Durand, *Recueil et parallèle des edifices de tout genre anciens et moderns, remarquables par leur beaute, parleur grandeur ou par leur singularite, et dessines sur une meme echelle* (Paris: Gillé, 1799).

9   Sergio Villari, *J. N. L. Durand (1760–1834): Art and Science of Architecture* (New York: Rizzoli International, 1990), 55.

10 Antoine Picon, "From 'Poetry of Art' to Method: The Theory of Jean-Nicolas-Louis Durand," in J. N. L. Durand, *Précis of the Lectures on Architecture; With Graphic Portion of the Lectures on Architecture* [1802] (Los Angeles: Getty Research Institute, 2000).

11 Durand, *Précis of the Lectures on Architecture*.

12 Quatremère, quoted in Vidler, *Writing of the Walls*, 152.

13 David Vanderburgh, "Typology," in *Encyclopedia of 20th-Century Architecture*, vol. 3, ed. R. Stephen Sennott (London: Fitzroy Dearborn, 2003), 1,356.

14 Aldo Rossi, *Architecture of the City*, trans. Diane Ghirardo and Joan Ockman (1966; Cambridge, Mass.: MIT Press, Oppositions Books, 1982). This is *L-architettura della citta*, the classic text that caused much excitement when it was translated into English.

15   Terence Goode, "Typological Theory in the U.S.: The Consumption of Architectural Authenticity," *Journal of Architectural Education* 46, no. 1 (1992): 2–13. Goode takes a somewhat controversial stance that links typological theory to postmodern pastiche.

16   Caniggia and Maffei, *Interpreting Basic Building*, 1–40.

17   Anne Vernez Moudon, "Getting to Know the Built Landscape: Typomorphology," in *Ordering Space: Type in Architecture and Design*, ed. Karen A. Franck and Linda Schneekloth (New York: Van Nostrand Reinhold, 1994). This is the authoritative history of the three movements—Italian, English, and French—of urban morphology.

18   Caniggia and Maffei, *Interpreting Basic Building*, 70–82.

19   Rob Krier, *Urban Space* (New York: Rizzoli, 1979).

20   Goode, "Typological Theory in the U.S."

21   Ibid.

22   M. R. G. Conzen, "Alnwick, Northumberland: A Study in Town-plan Analysis," publication no. 27 (London: Institute of British Geographers, 1960).

23   M. R. G. Conzen, "The Use of Town-plans in the Study of History," in *The Study of Urban History*, ed. H. J. Dyos (New York: St. Martin's Press, 1968), 114–30.

24   Léon Krier and Diru Thadani, *The Architecture of Community* (Washington, D.C.: Island Press, 2009).

CHAPTER 3: TYPOLOGICAL TRANSFORMATION

A building type can be described as an abstract characterization of a set of buildings that have common formal characteristics. Any particular building is just one instance or exemplar of the type. A building type is a formal configuration that constitutes a successful solution to a set of conditions that exist *at the moment that the first instance of the type evolved.* As long as the type comfortably matches the set of problems, it will continue to be repeated, with minor changes. At some point or under some circumstances, the type no longer fits as comfortably to the conditions, because the conditions change. It is then transformed—that is, the idea, not an actual building, is transformed. The next instance of its construction, as a type, reveals the evolution of a new form, perhaps only very slightly changed.

In this process of transformation, building types resemble organisms undergoing evolutionary processes. Organisms evolve when an accidental mutation presents a better survival response to the environment. Typological evolution is almost as spontaneous, but, of course, it is dependent on human agency. In the creation and evolution of building types, a particular type is successful when it responds to the conditions under which it is built. These immediate conditions exert influence but are not deterministic, since historic expectations, prior existence, and resistance to change are also "built into" the type.

Historic building types arose in the same way: in response to the conditions under which they were first built. These conditions include more than function. A train station type not only fulfilled the functions of buying and selling tickets, train arrival and departure, passenger waiting, loading and unloading, but also satisfied conditions of finance, profitability, siting, regulation, daily rhythms, and connections to other transport. No less important were the cultural conditions and expectations: Train stations were grand entrances to the city, measures of the wealth of the city, and indications of the extent of its transport network and the crowds attracted to it. Even more subtle were the generative conditions having to do with the desired symbolic link to a previous type, as train stations consciously imitated grand basilicas in order to establish their civic importance and scale (fig. 3-1). This cultural symbolism is not limited to 19th-century types: To

3-1 | Union Station, Washington, D.C., has been transformed into a shopping center, while retaining its function as a train station.

3-2 | *This is a suburban office building in San Antonio, Texas, but it could be anywhere.*

the extent that great halls in airports mimic the reception halls of grand train stations, they invoke a storied past and the idea of elegant and swift travel, and they complete a series of formal links (bathhouse–basilica–cathedral–train station–airport) that extends back to ancient times.[1]

A key idea in typology is that any given building type, such as a train station, develops certain common formal characteristics because, at certain periods of time, the conditions under which it arises and emerges are very much the same within extended geographic areas.[2] These common typological characteristics are self-reinforcing, so that at some point in time, building a train station comes to mean employing that building type as a shortcut to rethinking the entire design problem. Thus building types are tied to historical eras and to geographic and cultural areas.

Although monumental buildings of the past—for example, basilicas, theaters, and train stations—were usually expected to be architectural and stylistic variations on a set of understood types, modern monuments such as cathedrals and museums are more often interpreted as individual architectural constructions, not exemplars of a type. For this reason, type has come to be associated—erroneously—with imitating features of a historic building, and some designers think of the concept of type as applying only to historic buildings, not contemporary ones. To illuminate the concept of type used here and to understand the conditions that shape and define building types, a more prosaic and widespread contemporary example is used.

Alongside the interstate highways of most metropolitan areas is an array of multistory boxy buildings meant for office occupancy. This is the ubiquitous suburban office building. Architecturally, this type can be highly varied, but in its global form, it is quite repetitious, which is the hallmark of a type. The suburban office type is, formally, a low-rise building with a limited size footprint and an interior configuration with an elevator, service core, and hallways. These buildings are freestanding: unconnected to one another despite their proximity to one another and to other nearby uses (fig. 3-2). They cluster in groups of three or more on a site, and they are accessed almost entirely by car. Landscaped surfaces, parking lots, and sometimes a parking deck surround suburban office buildings. The floors of the suburban office building can be configured in a variety of ways, and they are occupied almost entirely by office uses, often by many different companies, with an occasional service such as a sandwich shop on the ground floor.

If building types are solutions to a set of conditions, what are the essential conditions that drive this common type? The first condition that must be recognized with any building type is the era in which it first comes to life and achieves typological status. The cultural and historical precedents of a type influence some of its characteristics. The office building is a relatively recent invention. Prior to the 19th century, most office functions were carried out in private homes or were attached to factories. The modern office building became popular in the mid-to-late 19th century, when the increasing scale of industrial functions made it necessary and convenient for office functions to be separated from the factory.[3] At the same time, technological changes in communications and construction—the invention of the telephone, the elevator, central heating, and steel structures—made multistory buildings attractive. Their downtown location was never questioned, as this was the central employment and transportation hub in every city. Even as streetcar suburbs were rapidly constructed and highway suburbs followed, office uses were predominantly downtown and the suburbs were mostly residential, with some convenience shopping.

Suburban office work locations at first were marginal—a couple of office floors in a neighborhood center, converted homes along a highway, or strip shopping centers converted to offices to satisfy a growing market. As the freeway system was built out, the suburban office type emerged, perhaps influenced by the campus ideas of a few innovative office complexes such as Frank Lloyd Wright's Johnson Wax project in Racine, Wisconsin. Unlike an urban center or even a neighborhood center, a campus office represented a place apart—isolated from the hubbub of the city—with dignity and identity. This notion fit very neatly with the idea of the suburb itself as a place of refuge and individual identity. The suburban office type thus took on some of the cultural character of the suburban residential neighborhoods, appealing to many of the executives who had relocated there.

Although early campus type buildings were innovative, the suburban office building soon settled into a very consistent and ubiquitous type. There are examples in every metropolitan area in the United States.

For the most part, these buildings were and are speculative; that is, the owner or developer of the building is not the tenant, and the building is leased, rather than sold to its user. Thus, the flexible internal arrangement of the suburban office type retains some similarity to its older typological cousin, the downtown high-rise office. This need for internal flexibility is a condition that drives many of the physical characteristics of the type, from open-structure floor plate, to central circulation cores, to the drop-in ceiling that conceals ducts and wires, to the standard floor-to-ceiling height (fig. 3-3).

The suburban office building type also reflects a set of very workable and convenient ideal dimensions. In the United States, we long ago standardized a narrow range of depth for efficient layout of offices. This depth accommodates a core; a hallway or two; a narrow interior zone for storage, support personnel, and circulation; and an exterior zone of offices or conference spaces that each boasts a window (fig. 3-4).

More informal formulas are involved in the length of the building, which is driven by building-code exiting requirements, maximum reasonable distance from the single or double elevator, and appropriate loading of elevators. It is not that a much longer or shorter building could not be designed or imagined, it is that such a deviation does not maximize the efficiency of the building. Efficiency here means the ratio of the necessary core and service spaces to the rentable areas.

The core is likewise designed to efficiently serve an exterior set of offices of a specific depth. It is designed to maximize required fire-exit circulation

3-3 | Variations on the suburban office building plan

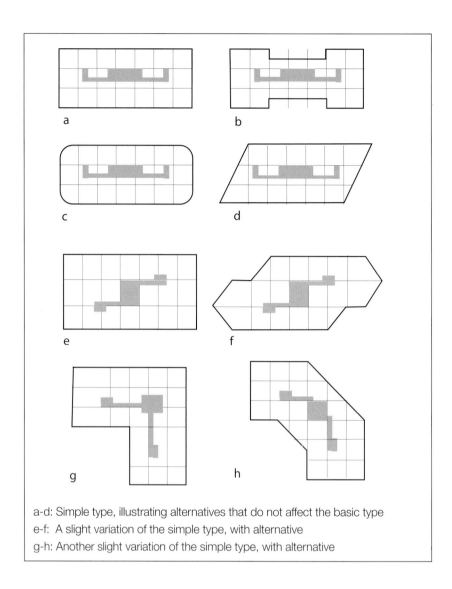

a-d: Simple type, illustrating alternatives that do not affect the basic type
e-f: A slight variation of the simple type, with alternative
g-h: Another slight variation of the simple type, with alternative

and net-to-gross ratios, while providing convenient demising, separating different businesses and providing an identity for each.

The type is the way it is and is repeated so often because *any other way does not fit the conditions as well.* Deviations from the formula impair the function, broadly defined as what the building is to *perform*.

TYPE IS RELATED TO FUNCTION

The function of a building is a more difficult concept than it first appears. One sense in which a building functions is that it easily accommodates, in spatial terms, the intended uses. In this example, the type accommodates a typical set of spaces associated with office occupation: private offices, conference rooms, reception areas, workrooms, kitchens, office cubicles, and so on. The suburban office building has a function not only in the sense of its use but also in terms of its economics. The building must generate money for its developer or owner. Many of the other attributes that a type embodies are also economically driven: They are formal characteristics that exist because the building has to be attractive enough to be desirable and competitive office space.

A key part of the formula is location. The suburban office type is rarely used in a rural location or in a downtown area. Most often this type is located on landscaped acreage, with good freeway access and visibility and convenient, highly visible, free parking (fig. 3-5). It is often surrounded by upscale housing subdivisions and some shopping. It is part of a standard package of the suburban lifestyle, designed to support convenient private auto use. It satisfies all kinds of businesses that do not depend on a central location. Because of the underlying land cost and simple construction, it is relatively inexpensive compared to office space in a central location. It is convenient to shopping, fast food, and other chains. It is convenient for auto commuters; convenient for the parking of users and guests; and accommodating of the single-person and single-vehicle modes of transport. It has easy delivery of business services, and it is easy to find.

Why is the suburban office building freestanding, instead of joined with others and arranged like a small village, which would make it more efficient to build and operate? Part of the answer is the marketing of the type. Each separate building is able to have a lead tenant with sign visibility from afar—ideally, from the freeway. (In some places, each side of a building has a different name.) A village configuration would not offer this individual identity and visibility, especially from the vantage point of the freeway. The landscaping around the building is also an identity issue. Landscaping of this lushness signals that the type is part of the suburban lifestyle, that there is ample land to separate the type from adjacent—possibly obnoxious—uses, and that it is not crowded. It is, in a sense, a "single-family office building," with its own lawn and clear demarcation of territory for the lead tenant. Landscaping signals that

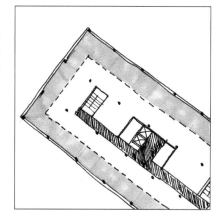

3-4 | Dimensions of a suburban office building's floor are somewhat standardized to accommodate the core, circulation, and inner and outer offices.

3–5 | A suburban office park with high visibility from the freeway, Salt Lake City

the building is more private and exclusive. Conversely, it also signals that the site is roomy and that plenty of parking is available so it can be visited easily.

Once a type has been established, its very success and its constant repetition generate certain meanings, symbolism, and expectations, which contribute substantially to the idea and continuity of the type, forming a self-reinforcing system. This typological idea is slowly embedded in the cultural understanding of what it means to inhabit and use the space, and what activities can be performed there and what cannot. The suburban office building type represents a standardized, predictable experience with few surprises or flourishes. The type boasts a staid, acceptable image—not too extravagant, not too cheap, not offbeat. It is safe, contemporary, and new— attracting the skittish suburban workforce that is uneasy with anything urban or inflected with a dodgy history or ethnicity.

The standardized form of the building type eventually inspires and directs the performances of all kinds of users. Visitors, for example, perform a well-choreographed, familiar dance: park, enter, orient, circulate vertically, check in, wait, have a meeting, part at the elevator, exit to the parking. The type is exquisitely evolved to respond to this dance and to support it, so much so that minor deviations of the type can be very vexing to users.

This visitor performance is an example of how the experience of the type reinforces the standard visitor experience and turns it into somewhat of a ritual. Perversely, the ritual could not exist in its precise form prior to the type that enables it. Parts of the ritual can endure even when the use of the building changes, because it is so tied to the physical characteristics of the type. Thus, an office building converted to a for-profit college will still inspire users (students) to perform the office building ritual, unless they are forcefully disrupted from doing so. Somewhat unconsciously, the office building type can heavily influence the meaning, experience, and rituals of the for-profit college users that occupy it, in strong contrast to the traditional campus rituals supported by academic building types.

The contemporary multiplex movie theater is another illustration of this ritual. Occupants learn their part in the "performance"—stand in line, move inside, buy refreshments, pass the ticket taker, orient, find the right auditorium, and select a seat—as it has been perfected by typological evolution. Familiarity with the performance and ritual supported by any given type is a cultural trope, making the experience of a new place—a movie theater in a different city, for example—more comfortable but less exciting.

The precise fine-tuning of the experience seems to most people to be a matter of "form follows function," which implies that the form is derived from the function precisely. It is more precise to say that a building type represents one specific and very limited interpretation of a series of functions that have been choreographed and refined over time, in part because of the existence of a successful type. The actual function—for example, watching a movie or running a law firm—can easily be accomplished in many different building forms that have little to do with the type. And many conditions, not just function, drive the form of building types.

NONTYPOLOGICAL CHARACTERISTICS

In the suburban office building type, there are critical conditions that generate the characteristics of the type: suburban location, low rise, attached surface or structured parking, undifferentiated floor plates with a compact core, standard column spacing, small ground-level lobby, generally square or rectangular shape with certain dimensional limits, many windows on the exterior, and a landscaped site. These characteristics are found in *all* exemplars of the type, by definition.

It is just as important to understand the characteristics of a building that are *not* typological. Within every type are examples with a wide variety of architectural expression, exterior and interior details, skin composition, materials and colors, stylistic flourishes, and small deviations in the shape of the building. These characteristics, in this case, are not typological.

Whatever is not necessary to precisely fulfill the conditions that define the type—function, site, location, economy, and generalized image in the case of the suburban office building—is eliminated from its essential definition. These are characteristics that are not common to all examples of the type. A particular roof shape, for example, is not a necessary component of the suburban office type. All examples of the type have additional characteristics. Any single exemplar will have particular design features and architectural expression. One suburban office building may have a hip roof, window louvers, skylights, brick details, and walnut interior doors. Endless other variations may be imagined and built. In fact, it is key to the concept of type that there is no such physical thing as a pure type, only examples that share common typological characteristics.

There is much individual variation—and occasional greatness—in the designs of particular instances of a given building type, but these have no significance in the definition or character of the type. Only when a particular design feature is repeated over and over in new exemplars of the type does it begin to reshape our idea of that type and suggest an evolution of the type itself.

In evolutionary terms, typological changes are adaptations that are successful. Over time, formal changes in the type all occur in this way. To the extent that these changes respond to changes in typological conditions, a variation may signal a slight transformation of the type, or it might become its own type. In the suburban office building, a common variation is an atrium (fig. 3-6). An atrium might have been a stylistic flourish at one point, but over time it could almost become a necessity in a particular area, because of refined conditions of marketing, social space, and so on. These new conditions generate new formal requirements, and to the extent that an atrium "solves" these requirements, it now becomes one of the defining characteristics of a new type.

The earlier type, the suburban office building without an atrium, may continue to be built in its old form or be completely supplanted by the new, evolved atrium type. In general, in the American urban landscape, variations that make the building type more financially sound will be adopted and

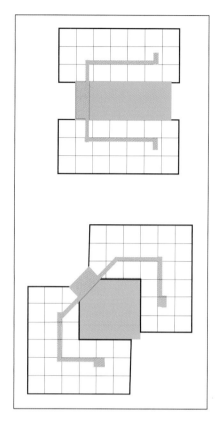

3-6 | Variations on the simple type to create an atrium building—usually a "doubling" of the simple type

replicated; those that do not will usually be discarded. This is because the values that drive speculative real estate development are heavily skewed toward economics, rather than some other value such as aesthetics, social networking, or green building. Successful adaptations may be local at first and competitive only within a specific region. Regional differences in types are very common.

VARIATION AND ADAPTATION

Some types are very resilient. The suburban office type appeared suddenly and has changed very little in the last 50 years. One would expect it to continue as long as the conditions that produced it stay nearly the same, but conditions can sometimes change dramatically without affecting a type very much. Partly this is because types represent a customary way of doing something, a way that is familiar for builders, predictable for lenders, and expected by businesses. Customary types exert a very strong resistance to change.

Designers also play a part in reinforcing type. Designing within a type means that many decisions have already been thought through and do not need to be reconsidered. Within the type, a designer might stretch some of the typological characteristics in order to more precisely satisfy a client's whim or another condition. For example, a designer might be interested in the following variations:

Image: To improve the image, add more landscaping or a bigger lawn, raise the height of the building, use better materials, add more architectural detailing, multiply the standard type into several related buildings, change the shape, or increase the floor-to-floor height.

Economy: To reduce cost, use only surface parking, eliminate unusual construction materials and detailing, make fewer floors with a larger floor plate, and use off-the-shelf building systems.

Individuality: To differentiate the "product," try an applied theme such as Georgian, old South, mountain chalet, or classic modern. Use arched windows or a copper roof.

Identity: To provide more external opportunities for business identity, make more than one circulation core or more than one entrance. Make the building's signs more integral to the building.

Sustainability: To reduce energy consumption, use more-efficient cladding materials, orient the building accordingly, try a more-efficient HVAC system or generate energy through photovoltaic panels, maximize natural light, use native landscaping and natural drainage, locate the building near a bus stop or trails, and add some bike racks.

Uses: Add nonoffice supporting uses such as a bank, day care, gym, coffee shop, business services, ATM, or delivery-service drop box.

All these variations can easily be accomplished while adhering to the standard type. And these are just variations that might be expected while maintaining the generative use as office occupancy. In the end, the suburban office type is very common because it is a very resilient type, easily modified to accommodate the changing needs of the office. In fact, its functional adaptability beyond office occupancy bodes well for long-term resilience of the type—if not any particular building.

Planners who are interested in limiting the proliferation of the type need to ask this question: Are there future conditions that might bring about a significant evolution or diminishment of this inherently useful and resilient type? Are there evolutionary steps to go from this type to another, more desirable one? Several scenarios can be imagined that would make the suburban office type obsolete or completely transform it. The most compelling and complete scenario would be the slow demise of the suburban lifestyle, especially a required reduction in personal automobile use such that people would have to walk or take transit to central or nodal locations rather than have access to decentralized types of any kind.

Far more likely are minor changes in conditions that might cause minor adaptations of the type. These include:

- the necessity for a much higher level of building security;
- regulation that requires higher density, connectivity, or mixed uses;
- significantly higher land costs that force higher density or taller buildings;
- greater availability of transit and competitive demand for it;
- the changing nature of office functions and rituals transforming the office into a combination coffee shop, gym, theme park, team room, teleconference space, movie house, 24–7 sleeping and work space, and hands-on lab for visual creativity, demonstration, and display;
- the changing nature of office workers because of the redefinition of hierarchies that eliminates support staff and equalizes job titles (and associated space), more creative modes of interaction, and shared job responsibilities; and,
- the changing need for permanent offices at all thanks to plug-and-play spaces in small satellites all over town instead of one central location, virtual-enabled home offices, or short-term accommodations for the home-office worker.

Because the space in the suburban office is so flexible, even these changes might not alter the basic type very much, as long as the suburban lifestyle remains compelling. Nevertheless, the office building itself is a relatively new type—perhaps only about 200 years old. Communication technologies perfected the downtown type as we know it, and our auto-centric lifestyle adapted the original type to become the suburban office building. It is not

3-7 | *Suburban office reused as a Baptist Church in Dallas*

a stretch to imagine that this type will become obsolete within 100 years, especially since the economic life of buildings that compose the type is fairly short, less than 30 years. After 30 years, these buildings typically have outlived their planned economic use, and any continued longevity is an economic surplus.

The fact that a type has become obsolete does not predict the fate of any particular building, which might be adaptable to many other uses. See, for example, the myriad adaptations of old-fashioned gas stations. Indeed, older exemplars of the suburban office building type are already being redeveloped and adapted for use as churches, lofts, and schools (fig. 3-7). This is another important mechanism of typological transformation. As old buildings are adapted successfully and repeatedly for new uses, the old type sometimes becomes associated with that new use. The conversion of 19th-century loft factories into loft housing is one example. This has been successful to the point that builders and designers are creating new lofts with many of the typological characteristics of old factory buildings. This fungibility of use is an illustration of why the idea of type, with its formal characteristics, can be separated from the precise function of a building.

THE MOST COMMON TYPE IN THE WORLD

Now we shall look at a type whose consistency over centuries is rather spooky. Figure 3-8 shows a reconstruction of a Roman *insula*, which initially appeared in the first or second century. The building is an apartment house built over a series of shops.[4] The apartments were a variety of sizes, and the configuration of the *insulae* varied according to the urban site available. "*Insula*" means "island" in Latin, and there is some dispute as to the origin of the word as a reference to this building type. Some archaeologists believe that it refers to individual apartments, but traditionally it is thought to mean

3-8 | *Reconstruction drawing of a Roman* insula, *from Ostia, circa 2nd century*

the entire block of the building, which might be completely surrounded by streets or public ways—an "island."[5]

I use *insula* here to refer to the type itself: an apartment building with wide openings on the ground floor, which is usually used for shops or workshops. Other characteristics of the type are the stairways leading to the upper floors from the street, the multiple bays of openings, the relative proportions of the upper and lower floor, their characteristic distinction and relationship, the openness of the ground floor, and the narrow range of variability of the width of the shop opening. Figures 3-9 to 3-12 depict a visual journey through time and space that reflect the dispersion of this type. Since no one has verified an actual dispersion, we are left with the important puzzle of whether

Left to right, top to bottom: 3-9 | Shrewsbury, England, circa 1900; 3-10 | Capen House, Boston, mid-19th century; 3-11 | Buildings from mid-19th century, Auburn, New York; 3-12 | Terre Haute, Indiana, 2000

3-13 | *Stoa of Attalus, Athens, Greece*

the *insula* was copied from place to place or whether it was independently derived in far different cultures over time.

We can only speculate that the first instances of this type were a typological evolution arising from two different original types: the single-story row of shops, which was surely refined from the Greek stoa or from a covered market stall; and the fancy Roman city home known as a *casa*, which sometimes boasted one or two shoplike spaces on the ground floor.

The stoa is an ancient type, a long covered building with one open side and a colonnade (fig. 3-13). The shop opened up to the colonnade. As the stoa type became more elaborate, the arcade became smaller and the enclosed shops deeper. It is not difficult to see that this type eventually evolved into the strip shopping center. In the *insula*, the shopkeeper often had a loft immediately accessible from inside the store where he or an employee could sleep and protect the merchandise. Perhaps this was an early innovation that then led to the idea of separate apartments above a row of shops. At some point, demand for land in a densely packed city led to the efficiency of multiple stories.

Each shop in the *insula* was a separate entity not connected to the upper floors. It was characterized by a wide opening directly onto the street or onto a continuous arcade. The opening at first was open air; as in a shopping mall, there was no barrier or permanent door. Large wooden doors or shutters were used to close the shop. Figure 3-14 is a 19th-century example from Thailand, where wooden doors are still used.

As the type moved into climates with less attractive weather, the large opening gave way to a storefront—a lightweight but permanent covering of the large opening, with a smaller door within it. This tradition of a lightweight opening within the frame of the building, which itself might be masonry or some other heavier material, survives as an architectural feature of the *insula*

3-14 | *At first, large wooden doors covered the openings of shops, as seen in these 19th-century examples that still remain in Thailand.*

Clockwise from above left: 3-15 | Insulae *in Aruba; 3-16 |* Shophouses, *a predominantly Asian variation of an* insula *type, in Singapore; 3-17 |* Insulae *in Buenos Aires, Argentina; 3-18 |* Insulae *in Cincinnati's Over-the-Rhine*

type. It has a similar function to the wide opening in that it minimally blocks the visual access—the view—into the shop. Therefore, it would not be typologically correct to fill in the large opening of a shop front with masonry or other heavy material, although this is a common violation of the type.

For reasons that we can only speculate on, the agreed size of the opening of a storefront, sometimes called a bay, ranges between 10 and 15 feet. Only the most recent examples are larger than this. The most convincing explanation is structural: Spanning a larger opening with a single lintel was likely impractical without contemporary materials. Even today, a shopkeeper can easily keep track of the goings and comings of customers with a relatively modest opening, which might not be possible with a larger one. And it is also possible that, as modern mall designers realize, narrower openings create an interesting experience with a row of shops that have variety and entice customers to keep walking along the street.

This type, of course, survives today almost unchanged except for technological innovations such as the elevator, plate glass, aluminum storefronts, and indoor plumbing. In its journey, the type has dispersed to almost every culture, continent, and era on Earth (figs. 3-15 to 3-18). There are examples from medieval times to the 20th century, from Asia to Brazil. The variations are endless, but the consistency of the type over two millennia is quite remarkable.

The persistence of the *insula* and other similar types raises an interesting question: Is this type resilient because of its pedigree, or through imitation, or because it has some relationship to the natural proclivities of humans? Did we stumble on, or refine, a type that perfectly relates to our natural selves:

3-19 | *An evolution of the type in one location*

physical stature and gait, curiosity, need for variety and stimulation in order to buy, and need for a complement of housing of reasonable scale for an urban habitation. Linguistics has found certain formations of language to be universal. Are building types such as the *insula* in any sense universal? That is, are they innate, genetically generated types that reoccur from culture to culture? Or, paralleling a theory in linguistics, do types arise from lived experience that is comparable from culture to culture?

Over time, the *insula* type family has branched in response to changing conditions. Beginning in the 19th century, the type grew in height and needed slight changes to accommodate a proper lobby, instead of just a set of stairs, for the control and influx of more people living above. Also, in the 18th and 19th centuries, the type spawned a new variety that brought offices and factories to the upper floors instead of apartments. Elevators, electricity, and communications greatly expanded the height potential and shifted the more expensive units to the top of the building instead of closer to the ground.

Another branch of the family has a single bay rather than multiple bays. Responding to the narrow lots that characterized many of the American gridded cities, this probably began as a single house that was torn down to become a shop with a residence above, as city traffic justified it and as living on the ground floor became unpleasant. Figure 3-19 shows the evolution of this single-shop type over time in one neighborhood: As the neighborhood, in Cincinnati's Over-the-Rhine, became more prosperous, the wood houses, like the one on the left, were replaced by successively taller and more substantially built exemplars. Note that these buildings all still occupy their original narrow lots, which are 25 feet wide and 100 feet deep.

3-20 (left) | The insula *type in New Orleans, with an applied balcony and doors opening onto the balcony on upper floors*

3-21 (above) | *This* insula *in Thailand has a balcony integrated into the mass.*

3-22 (below) | *A contemporary variation of the* insula *that really constitutes a new type: a multi-floor store and a penthouse for office use*

Another variation has a balcony or arcade along the front, shown here in examples from New Orleans (fig. 3-20) and Thailand (fig. 3-21). This variation is as old as the type itself. It is climatically generated and occurs in warm climates where the shade of an arcade on the ground floor is just as welcome as the outdoor balcony on upper floors.

The San Francisco example in Figure 3-22 is a more recent innovation, with a single shop spanning several floors. This time, the designer has modified the typological convention of a series of wide openings on the ground floor and instead created a large expanse of glass on the upper floor—while still maintaining the base-middle-top formula common in architectural composition. It makes sense to do this if the upper floor is the penthouse; in the traditional *insula* type, the top-floor walk-up is the least desirable and often has low ceilings and small windows. The openings on the ground floor are more consistently related to the middle floor, showing us on the outside that the store is, in fact, on several floors. Note the corner conditions, with rounded windows. This is a common regional variant in San Francisco, like a contemporary bay window.

This is a good example of how a designer can manipulate our common understanding of the type to invoke a completely different idea. This designer successfully plays on a confused reading—is it a large grand house or a store?—to suggest that it may be something it is not: an expensive single-family town house converted to a very exclusive store. It is also an example of how types shift in response to technological change, in this case, a transformation due to the increasing importance of the top floor as elevators made it possible for elites to enjoy fresh breezes, better views, and less noise.

Some types require a technological innovation to be born, and others die out for the same reason. The *insula* type itself was a multistory building that required structural innovation by Roman engineers, if not perfection: Shoddy construction caused the collapse of many *insulae*. Being densely occupied and without heat, they were also frequently subject to destruction by fire.

Nevertheless, the *insula* type was very constant through history before the automobile changed the equation of walking distance, street frontage, view into the shop, a walking gait, and a human scale of signs, openings, and windows. The rise of the personal automobile was an extremely compelling force; in places built after its dispersion, all earlier common types were substantially adapted to meet its requirements, and some types simply became obsolete.

The *insula* type, so important for centuries, almost completely ceased being built in the wake of the automobile, especially in suburban areas where new construction dominated. The primary reason was the dispersion characteristic of the auto culture: Spreading out obviated the need to stack housing on top of shops, and the shops needed much more space for parking. At some point, the shops became much larger. Since they no longer were restricted to a walking-only clientele, they could expand their market area to many square miles. Motorized transport also changed how distribution systems worked, drawing goods from distant lands instead of close to the shop. As the entire system changed, the type—so finely tuned to a small-scale but dense and pedestrian way of life—disappeared wherever car culture dominated.

Because of this type's close association with dense but small-scale pedestrian living and local distribution, it has taken on new meaning in the post-auto context. This is an example of how designers appropriate a type in order to invoke its embedded associations. In this case, new urbanists have appropriated this type as a shorthand for urbanity of a certain moderate scale. Not only is it is immediately recognizable as a culturally ancient type, it is also comfortably low scale: not a high-rise apartment or other skyscraper that has different and less homey associations. It appears, as it always has, to be a part of an intimate-scale neighborhood. Our almost involuntary recognition of this type and its associations lends legitimacy to the new urbanist agenda but also allows activists to encourage a particular scale of development on a hesitant public used to much more dispersed conditions.

This time, instead of being resultant of cultural and economic conditions, the *insula* type is used as an ideal, in service to the idea of a compact, walkable neighborhood (fig. 3-23). The type invokes an urban building block, taking the historic city as the ideal, with the result that there is a "wrong" way and a "right" way to build this new type, as it must be used properly to invoke the right kind of urban performance.

When new urbanists invoke the *insula*, they are summoning up one of the richest, most ancient examples of type in the world, illustrating how meaning is embedded in types. Customary associations develop over time that are as complex as any kind of relationship. As participants in a culture, we learn these associations and behaviors as a part of everyday life. Just as

everyone knows the particular performance that is required to seamlessly operate a suburban office building, we also have an underlying sense of the kind of businesses that thrive there and expectations of their size, economic stature, characteristic employees, and daily habits. All of these associations, developed over time, enrich our idea of type so that it becomes much more than a three-dimensional diagram.

GAS STATIONS AND FAST-FOOD RESTAURANTS

Most types transform slowly over time, and some, such as the *insula*, are barely changed over a millennium. Since the invention of the car culture, there has been an explosion of new types. Some examples include shopping centers, big box stores, airports, gas stations, and fast-food restaurants. These types have arisen and evolved so quickly that it is possible to see the transformation simply by observing several examples that were built only a few years apart. This allows us to study the nature of transformation itself.

One of the most fascinating types to watch is the fast-food restaurant building. Several innovations in management and food-service technology were required to actualize the type. At first the business was only for a self-service walk-up clientele. McDonald's, for example, began franchising stores in 1953, but its first drive-through was not built until 1975.[6] In the meantime, several enterprising chains had claimed the drive-through mantle, including Jack in the Box, which capitalized on this model of business. The evolution of this type, therefore, moved quickly from a drive-up freestanding building with a walk-up window, to a building with an interior counter only, to a building with an interior counter and drive-through, and most recently to the drive-through with interior

3-24 | *The first McDonald's (1955) was a walk-up restaurant, as seen in this reconstruction in Des Plaines, Illinois.*

3-25 | *Design details of the standard contemporary drive-through type are adapted for the desert landscape of Phoenix, Arizona.*

3-26 | *McDonald's adapted the type with an add-on of an indoor playground. This one is literally added to an older store.*

counter and interior seating that is familiar to people worldwide today (figs. 3-24 to 3-26).

This rapid evolution was driven by the equally rapid changes in the culture. Although the concept of take-out food existed as far back as the first century—Pompeii boasted an open-air take-out counter—the 20th-century innovation in fast food was made-to-order food that was served within a few minutes. This occurred almost simultaneously with the rapid expansion of the car culture, which led to suburban expansion. In the suburbs, it was possible to have inexpensive land to build a drive-though lane, and the traffic flow allowed one to move more freely than in congested cities.

Suburbs also meant longer commutes, and with more women in the workforce, fast food rose in popularity as a convenient substitute for the housewife's home-cooked meal. The adaptation of the drive-though window was a natural next step: no need to leave the children in the car to dash in and order a meal to go.

And as long as you are dragging the children along . . . a variation on this type now provides extensive indoor playgrounds for children. Fast food became strongly associated with children after special "happy meals" were created in the 1980s.

Even though the fast-food restaurants have strong brand distinction, the modern type is nearly indistinguishable from one franchise to the other, demonstrating that the resolution of forces that create the type are similar and also that they are subject to expectations that derive from one another. Successful adaptations are quickly adopted across all chains.

Gas stations are another type that has undergone rapid change in the 20th century. Old-fashioned stations were not much more than a couple of pumps on the side of the road, perhaps with a small building and canopy to drive under (figs. 3-27 and 3-28). Service bays became common as gas stations expanded their line of business.[7] In time, more service bays and canopies were added, and the sprawling station with many vehicles pulling in and out nearly always required a corner site (fig. 3-29). The introduction of credit cards and self-service changed the nature of the business, too. In a 1970s evolution, the gas station combined with a convenience store to offer one-stop shopping for snacks and sundries (fig. 3-30). Gas-station personnel became shopkeepers instead of car experts. Shortly afterward, service bays disappeared as specialty tire, battery, and oil change shops opened; a new type was spawned that has a compelling similarity to an old gas station.

Another recent evolution of the gas station is a subtle one: The orientation of the canopies and the rows of pumps has shifted 90 degrees, so that the cars now pull up perpendicular to the store, instead of parallel to it. Market studies show that this arrangement is more conducive to customers getting out of cars and going into the store. This minor shift draws attention to the minute and very precise adaptations that are a part of refining this type and many others.

In the past few years, gas stations have evolved again, becoming adjuncts to big box stores; they are nothing but a canopy and pumps. A

3-27 (top) | Early gas stations like this one in Commerce, Oklahoma, were not much more than a pump.

3-28 (middle) | A well-preserved station in Ohio

3-29 (bottom) | Gas-station types had service bays until the mid-1980s. Older types such as this one in Carver, Minnesota, have now been repurposed to serve as specialty shops for mufflers, brakes, and oil changes.

3-30 (top) | Contemporary stations, such as this Chevron one in Virgin, Utah, often have a convenience store.

3-31 (bottom) | The newest stations, like this one at a Sam's Club in Salt Lake City, are not much more than pumps—again.

single employee sits in a tiny building, monitoring but not attending the customers, who make their transactions without assistance (fig. 3-31).

And what will come next? If electric cars become common, the "gas station" might become a place to charge your vehicle or to exchange your battery. If car-sharing services become popular, stations might evolve into car pick-up and storage centers. In either case, the type may sprout more social spaces associated with waiting for a service to be completed.

It is the restless and constant adaptation of our contemporary types that makes them so interesting. We are in a state of change; conditions that can have enormous impact on all urban types, not only fast food, are just over the horizon.

ENDNOTES

1   Aldo Rossi first made the connection of these building types in his classic book, *Architecture of the City,* which for many architects was an awakening to the power of form types: Aldo Rossi, Architecture of the City, trans. Diane Ghirardo and Joan Ockman (1966; Cambridge, Mass.: MIT Press, Oppositions Books, 1982).

2   Gianfranco Caniggia and Gian Luigi Maffei, *Interpreting Basic Building: Architectural Composition and Building Typology* [1979], trans. Susan Jane Fraser (Florence: Alinea Editrice, 2001). This text, finally translated in 2001, remains the key guide to the typological theory promoted in this book.

3   Sir Nikolaus Pevsner, *A History of Building Types* (London: Thames and Hudson, 1976): 213–25.

4   James Packer, *The Insulae of Imperial Ostia* (Rome: American Academy in Rome, 1971). Packer's classic text extensively documents and interprets the archaeological record of *insulae* found in Ostia, Italy.

5   Glen Storey, "The Meaning of Insula in Roman Residential Terminology," in *Memoirs of the American Academy in Rome* (Ann Arbor, Mich.: University of Michigan Press for the American Academy in Rome, 2004), 49:47.

6   The first McDonald's drive-through was built in Sierra Vista, Arizona, to accommodate fatigue-clad soldiers from a nearby fort, who were not to appear in public. See www .roadsideamerica.com/tip/9530 and www.mcdonalds.com/us/en/our_story/our_history .html.

7   John A. Jakle and Keith A. Sculle, *The Gas Station in America* (Baltimore: Johns Hopkins University Press, 1994).

CHAPTER 4: TYPOLOGY AND URBAN TRANSFORMATION

The built artifacts of the city—its buildings, bridges, streets, built landscape, and other visible objects—have the greatest impact on our senses. It is tempting and common to study types and other artifacts as game pieces to move around in order to create better cities.

Recently, a young designer lectured at my school about a plan that he was proposing to add density to a suburban housing subdivision. In this plan, he had considered the existing houses as permanent objects that needed to remain. He proposed that new residential types be squeezed in between the houses, behind the houses, and in the space of the streets and rights-of-way.

On paper, this plan seems sound, but it ignores the hard reality of land ownership: buildings and even building types are rather ephemeral, but the urban tissue—streets and lots—is persistent. Street rights-of-way and property lines will endure for centuries, while buildings come and go. Even a cataclysmic event such as a widespread fire, a natural disaster, or a war will not usually alter the underlying and invisible web of property boundaries. The space of the city is completely divided up in this invisible web. There is no land, not even the space of the street, that is not primarily owned or controlled by some entity, whether a government, other organization, or an individual (fig. 4-1).

The property boundaries are the actual game board for all urban action, including planning proposals. All plans, ideas, building construction, demolition, and changes in type or use are carried out within the lines of this game board. For the most part, except for regulation, all significant proposals require the consent of property owners, or they require that the property be acquired through some means. Regulation assumes the unit of measure of the property boundary, not the buildings.

4-1 | *This cadastral map shows only the property lines and reveals how the entire space of the city is claimed by owners.*

BUILDING TYPES AND URBAN TISSUES

Urban *tissue* is the term that urban morphologists use to describe the arrangement of lots, blocks, and streets, or the demarcation of the owned

4-2 | *The underlying plan of Charleston, South Carolina, gives order to the buildings and to consistent building types, as in many historic districts.*

space of the city. Sometimes it is called the urban fabric. It is possible to think of a particular tissue as being a type—at a different scale from the building type but related to it.

Common building types arise within the context of a particular kind of urban tissue. A single-family house type—for example, a four square—fits precisely on a particular size lot within a street and block pattern. That is because the tissue was actually planned and created to support that type and others of its scale. In places that are planned, there is a congruency between the original type that was expected to be built and the original tissue that was created.

Urban coherence depends on a certain degree of typological consistency. Most designers instinctively understand that the patterns of buildings and open spaces that make up an urban environment are fundamental to the creation and preservation of a consistent context.

When confronted with an unusually consistent historic urban environment—say, the French Quarter of New Orleans—we admire the old buildings and their architectural details but often fail to realize that a large part of the charm is the relationship of the buildings to the street and the consistency of the building types. Though not all the same, they share certain characteristics.

Just as important, these types are built within a consistent pattern of lots, blocks, and streets. It could be argued that in virtually all of our most admired historic areas—Charleston, South Carolina; Beacon Hill, Boston; San Francisco—it is the underlying pattern of streets, lots, and blocks that give rise to and continue to moderate these consistent building types. Architectural styles and details enrich this pattern but are not sufficient in themselves to create the atmosphere that these places invoke (fig. 4-2).

A grid of streets with blocks subdivided into lots underlies nearly all American cities (fig. 4-3), with a few notable exceptions that were typically older and grew without a plan at first—Boston and New York are prominent examples. After almost two centuries of unplanned development in New York City, the 1811 Commissioners Plan was established. It laid out an ambitious and famous grid of streets (fig. 4-4). The standard block width did not vary significantly anywhere in the plan, a width that was just right for the depth of the most common building types and lots of the day. Surveyors assumed that the common type would be built—they knew no others that were appropriate— and even though it took many decades to build far north into Harlem, most of the city was indeed built out with a few different but related types.

Even villages and cities that grew without a plan usually assumed a common urban type as new streets and properties were successively added.[1] An "unplanned" city is actually not unplanned, of course, it is just that the increment of the plan is much smaller: for instance, a person dividing up his own property and adding it to a preexisting network, even if that network is composed of cow paths or, more commonly, country roads.[2]

The traditional relationship of original building type to the original network of lots, blocks, and streets continues today in all housing subdivisions, which

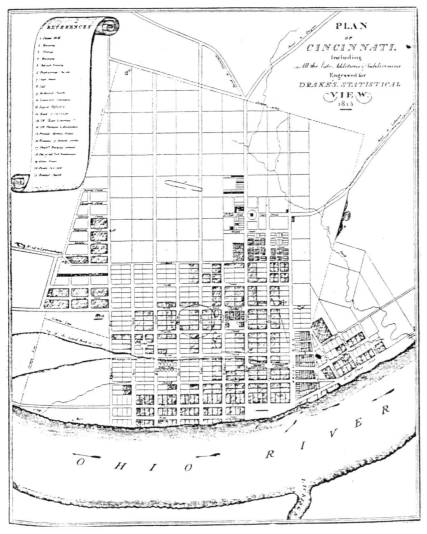

4-3 | A regular pattern of lots and blocks characterized the founding of most towns in the United States. Cincinnati, in 1815, is shown growing into the fields, known as outlots, that were established north of the city.

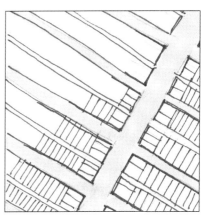

4-4 | New York's grid was established in 1811, with blocks of a consistent width but of varying lengths. The width of the block corresponded to the depth of common lots and building types of the era. Slight variations in the lot width from block to block arose as the blocks were developed over time.

are precisely planned to accommodate contemporary houses, according to the expectations of the future residents—known as "the market"—and the allowable metrics given in regulation. Each house and its driveway, yards, and garage, sits on its own separate plot of land. Although there were some experiments in communally owned property for single-family houses in the 1920s, the concept never caught on, despite the interesting urban plans and open spaces that were afforded by this idea.[3] The divided form of ownership actually strengthens the neighborhood by making it very difficult to make radical changes. The smaller the pieces and the more widely distributed they are in ownership, the more difficult it is to propose a grand scheme, to the point that it actually becomes impossible without enormous top-down effort.[4]

That is not to say that neighborhoods such as those in New York City, New Orleans, or contemporary suburbs do not undergo transformation over time. Owners are constantly improving their individual properties with additions, renovations, and other changes. A few decades after the origin of the place, buildings start to be routinely torn down and replaced, or transformed beyond recognition in accordance with the typological transformation processes that have already been described. More resilient types will be adapted. Less resilient ones—often, larger and more specialized buildings—will be torn down and replaced with a modern type. Given the regulatory freedom to do so, owners in places on the upswing will respond to real estate pressures by building more densely on the same lot, through greater lot coverage, taller buildings with more floors, or both. Less commonly, an owner will buy the lot next door and build a larger building on two or more lots.

Although traditionally and historically this is a very common process of transformation in cities, it runs into some difficulty in the suburbs, where combining lots and building a much larger house—or a "monster home"—is viewed as an offense to the context of the neighborhood. Many inner-ring suburbs are fighting this trend rather than viewing it as a normal urban transformation.[5] In Houston, where zoning is rare, it is possible to find entire streets of large homes that have been incrementally built on lots that once housed small cottages.[6] This remarkable transformation took a little over a decade.

4-5 | Single-family housing developments, such as this one in Colorado Springs, Colorado, are examples of static tissues.

In properties where values are slipping, on the other hand, a different transformation sometimes occurs. Owners do not invest in improvements, and they allow buildings to deteriorate. Properties that are difficult to maintain or rent are torn down or rebuilt as different types with more economic possibility: a storage yard, a parking lot, or a repair shop, for example. Over time, the neighborhood becomes pocketed with vacant land. In an interesting twist, the difficulty of bringing it back is also complicated by the dispersed ownership pattern. It turns out that this tissue structure retards change in both positive and negative ways.

These two different patterns of transformation are both termed "organic" by morphologists, who see the small-scale constant change as akin to an organism's ability to change with tiny, almost invisible adaptations over great periods of time. These small adaptations are conditioned and constrained by the relatively small-scale tissue that had a somewhat orderly origin.[7] Under the schema of organic transformation, the tissue must provide a very precise, small-scale, and consistent underlying order so that change is not dramatic or disruptive but smooth and constant.

Tissues like this are termed "static." Static tissues are characteristically more ordered than other tissues, and they form a consistent pattern. Most urban grids and all planned single-family subdivisions are examples of static tissues (fig. 4-5). Static tissues have lots and streets that were planned together, surveyed at about the same time, and originally built on within a period of 10 to 20 years. The lots are relatively small and are roughly the same size within the area of the tissue. Importantly, the lots usually contain a single major structure of a type that is congruent with the plan of the tissue—that is, the tissue itself was originally expected to accommodate this particular type of structure—and subsequent transformations have been accommodated within the basic module of the tissue.

Because property ownership is highly protected by the state and by the owner himself, the static tissue is a very stable and persistent element of urban form. The relatively small size of the lots in a static tissue indicates a divided form of ownership and management that resists wholesale change by lot aggregations. Too, these forms tend to be protected through zoning regulation that prevents further subdivision. The rapid build out of these tissues tends to favor very consistent building types. Consistency of type tends to stabilize the area: Redevelopment that is inconsistent with the existing fabric is discouraged because it is less marketable and has a chilling effect on nearby property values.

Static tissues are the most stable urban form that exists: They allow change to happen but only in small increments that are somewhat consistent with the original types. Although there can be growing pains in this urban formation, its consistency is self-reinforcing (fig. 4-6).

There are two other kinds of tissues that dominate the American landscape. Although static tissues are very common in older places, these other two reached a zenith in the 20th century.[8] The first of these is called a *campus* tissue: a larger tract of land with multiple buildings, owned by

4-6 | *The single-family housing tissues in these examples from Hudson, Ohio, have transformed in size and configuration over time. They are shown at the same scale.*

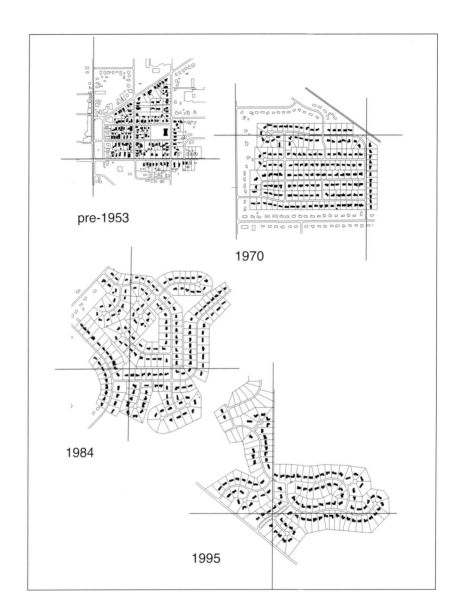

pre-1953

1970

1984

1995

a single entity (fig. 4-7). Examples are apartment complexes, universities, airports, large hospitals, industrial parks, and shopping centers. The defining characteristic of a campus tissue is that the lot is not subdivided when new buildings are added or changed. Campus tissues contain more than one significant building and usually have an internal circulation system of roads and paths that connect the buildings. They are usually somewhat physically isolated from other tissues nearby and not connected to a network of streets, except at limited entrances.

The final dominant tissue type is the least stable of the three tissue formations: the *elastic* tissue. Elastic tissues typically form along arterial roads and have a rapid change rate compared to static tissues (fig. 4-8). Their characteristics include the following: a great variety of lot

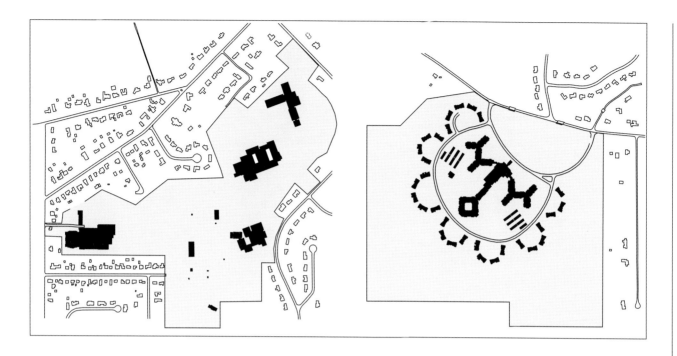

4-7 | Two examples of a campus tissue: a school complex on the left and an apartment project on the right.

sizes, many different building types in close proximity, and a paucity of street networks.

The elastic tissues pose a great many problems since they are so fundamentally disordered. Lots tend to range from very large to very small, with a wide variation in size. The tissues have little or no pattern since they are created directly by subdivision of individual farm fields or aggregation of small pre-urban roadside houses, without the establishment of a road network. Development of the tissue thus relies heavily on a single arterial road, which receives tremendous traffic as a result. Finally, highly varied lots within the tissue support a wide variety of building types that are not only inconsistent with one another but may have no logical orientation or scale relationship to the lot and the street.

Chapter 6 discusses the campus and elastic tissues and their transformational characteristics in more detail.

TYPOLOGY AND URBAN TRANSFORMATION: ORIGIN AND DISRUPTION

Historically, static tissues constituted the largest group of tissue types in the city. Even in a city that grew organically—without a plan—the building lots of the city were created with specific types in mind. Those types were limited in size and scale and mostly presumed to be joined types that would form an urban street wall. This was simply the most efficient way to build, maximizing the space of a precious urban lot and minimizing the walking distance in cities, where distance to the center was critical to any property.

Most of the time, these were ordinary building types, the kind that house the shops, workshops, and residences of the majority of people.

4-8 | *Elastic tissues are irregular formations of land subdivisions that give rise to irregular buildings without typological consistency.*

The handy *insulae* type was one of these, as were simple row houses and courtyard types. By building on lots that were nearly the same size and had a consistent street-frontage width, builders created static tissues with similar typologies right up until the car culture intervened dramatically in the 1940s.

Static tissues were also formed in several other ways, including planned districts such as New Town in Edinburgh, Scotland, and Savannah, Georgia, or the planned grids of most center cities in the American West. Incremental growth can also form static tissues, such as a grid extension out from a central grid. The grid extension may be somewhat haphazard compared to the original city, but the lots and blocks that are subdivided and added to the city are nevertheless static tissues built for a particular type.

While most towns were at first grown by extending the grid system, many were prevented from these logical extensions by a preexisting pattern of farm lots, or outlots, that were established as part of the original plat. Figure 4-3 shows the outlots in Cincinnati to the north of the urban grid. These places were originally intended as convenient farm and livestock plots for town residents, and they also housed the more noxious uses associated with towns, such as blacksmiths and stables. As cities grew, outlots were subsumed into the urban network, but their contrasting origin meant that a completely different pattern was injected into the grid.

It turns out that the original pattern of a tissue has a very long-lasting effect on the subsequent development patterns, affecting the neighborhood's longevity, stability, consistency, and ability to change. Because tissues are extremely persistent structures, they tend to retard change. But if they are disordered in their origins, they also encode that disorder for a very long time, if not forever. Likewise, if the tissue is orderly to begin with, as most static tissues are, it also encodes that order for a very long time.

The historic neighborhood of Over-the-Rhine, in Cincinnati, is an example of an extension of a city's original downtown grid. Originally platted as large outlots used for crops and noxious industries, the area was developed with urban uses starting in the early 19th century. This was accomplished by the separate action of each outlot owner, who subdivided his lot in whatever way was convenient. Even with this lack of coordination, the subdivided lots all had a very similar size: 25 feet wide and about 125 feet deep. This size was the optimum dimension for the most common urban type being built then in North America: a single-bay tenement house that had a store on the bottom level and two, three, or four floors of apartments above (fig. 4-9).

Even though the pattern of lots was somewhat haphazard, where the lots had regularity within a block the area prospered and was built out more quickly. In blocks where owners chose not to subdivide in advance but to sell off parcels one at a time, development was slower and the building types were not as consistent.

By 1855, the district was fully built out with moderately sized types that fit neatly on the lots, with plenty of backyard space for the kinds of shop, livery, and gardening activities that were common (fig. 4-10). But a remarkable transformation in the neighborhood had occurred by 1875: Almost every building had been torn down and replaced with a larger, better built, and more prestigious structure. The immigrants who had

4-9 | Main Street in Over-the-Rhine, Cincinnati, with buildings surviving from the 1870s

4-10 | *The evolution of Over-the-Rhine, Cincinnati, from 1855 to 1991 captures the slow changes that occur in a neighborhood, including a densification from 1855 to 1891. A slow dissolution from 1955 to 1991 left wide vacancy. The lower diagram shows the original outlots and the subdivision for urban development.*

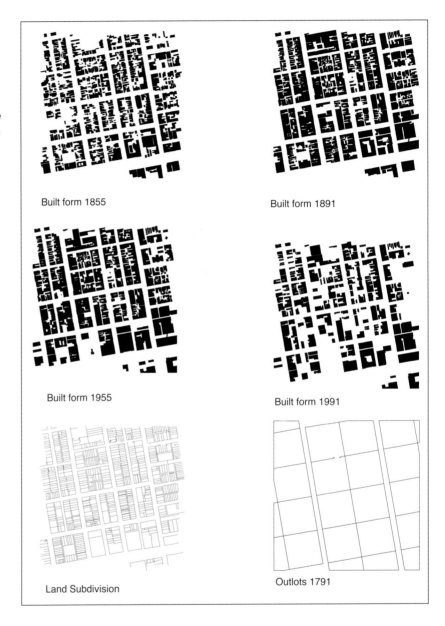

Built form 1855

Built form 1891

Built form 1955

Built form 1991

Land Subdivision

Outlots 1791

pioneered this part of town had prospered over the years and were now able to rebuild in a substantial way.

Typologically, the new buildings were very similar to the ones torn down. Because they needed to fit within the existing lots, they followed a very similar type, albeit much grander. Figure 4-11 captures the kind of transformation that might have happened: The building on the left is of the wooden type originally built, the middle one is brick and slightly larger, and the one on the right is an exemplar of the later substantial type.

The grand buildings remained in place for decades despite many forces of change in the neighborhood, including a significant population shift in the

4-11 | The evolution of a type, from left to right: from the earliest rough wooden construction, to slightly more substantial, to the latest four-story incarnation. Note that the lot size is the same.

1930s that drove out original owner-residents and created a ghetto of poor Appalachian and African-Americans. In 1955, most of the substantial types were still standing, and even today a large number of them are hanging on, awaiting a revival that always seems just out of reach.

In a study of this neighborhood, Daniel Ferdelman and I explored the idea of persistence, the idea that certain kinds of urban formations are more stable and therefore last longer in time.[9] Morphologists have determined many times that streets—not the paving itself, but the paths—are very persistent. In Florence, Italy, ancient Roman streets are readable despite 2,000 years of development and change. The only thing left of lower Manhattan from a map in 1660 is the space of the streets, which remain almost exactly as they were then. In 1660, Wall Street followed a defensive wall, Broadway was rather wide, and Canal Street sported a canal (fig. 4-12).

Streets are notoriously difficult to change, because they are the boundaries of property and they constitute the access to property that is essential for development. In modern days they also contain utilities and other public services, and that increases the cost of shifting the location of a street even a few feet.

It turns out that property lines are very persistent, too. The study of Over-the-Rhine, Cincinnati, where a single neighborhood was followed for almost 200 years, found that the property lines, once laid down,

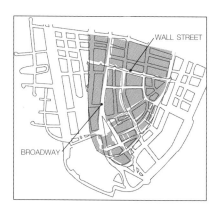

4-12 | An overlay of two maps of lower Manhattan—one from 1660 and one from 1995. Broadway, Canal Street, and Wall Street (with wall) remain in the same location. Note the expansion of land over time.

were almost never erased. However, it is relatively common for lots to be subdivided or to be adjoined so that two or more lots create a new, larger parcel. This system tends to make the development modular where property is similar in dimension to begin with. On the other hand, it is very rare that a district or place is recast with a different subdivision pattern once one has been laid down.

In Over-the-Rhine, the underlying tissue created a framework so that orderly change could happen quickly and without significant disruption to the operation and everyday life of the neighborhood. The original wooden tenement types in Over-the-Rhine gave way to larger, more durable buildings in a transformation that echoes through time. The building types were allowed to transform in a way that was dramatic and necessary, but the underlying tissue stayed the same.

This transformational process is not as well understood as it could be. Much of Over-the-Rhine was destroyed in the last half of the 20th century as institutions such as schools and courthouses gobbled up adjacent land, streets were widened, and much larger housing projects were built to replace the now-dilapidated 19th-century types. Not only were fine historic exemplars destroyed, but the combining of lots for larger uses affected the underlying tissue, making the orderly transition that occurred in the 19th century no longer possible.

Without an intact underlying tissue, one reasonable strategy for planning intervention or even spontaneous regeneration fades away: creation and promotion of a contemporary type that would fit into the same lot space as the old types. A new type could address contemporary needs such as parking and modern family living arrangements. This new type might be the 21st-century equivalent of the more durable type built in the 19th century. It would also fit seamlessly next to surviving older types.

The study of Over-the-Rhine also uncovered that the standard 19th-century type was considerably more durable and thus more likely to have survived the 150-year span. As Rossi points out, types tend to persist even when the buildings themselves are replaced.[10] In Over-the-Rhine, almost all the buildings were replaced between 1855 and 1891, yet the standard type was the same, although enlarged and made of more substantial materials than the original wooden structures.

Only the larger, less flexible buildings—hospitals, schools—were subject to widespread destruction, while the smaller standard-type buildings were able to adapt successfully to new changes. These buildings have several qualities that help them survive the natural selection process this implies. First, they are relatively small and require a small investment to be altered and adapted, compared to the vast capital required for larger renovations. Second, they have always been used primarily for housing, a land use that is never obsolete. Third, they are quite flexible in their interior arrangement and built of materials that are easily altered. Fourth, their individuality as buildings makes them readily available for a single owner to purchase and renovate.

A GRID TOO BIG: SALT LAKE CITY

Salt Lake City was founded and laid out in 1847 by Brigham Young, then the leader of the Mormon Church. The basic plan had a very large grid (660 feet square) with wide streets (132 feet). It was derived from a much earlier plan, a holy revelation, by Joseph Smith, the founder of the religion. That earlier plan was envisioned for Zion, a city proposed for Missouri that was to become the center of the Church's gathering on Earth. It was never built.

The unusual dimensions of the plat of Salt Lake City had tremendous repercussions for its development, but it was not the dimensions of the blocks and streets that were the most troublesome. Brigham Young divided up each of these large blocks into only eight lots, though Joseph Smith had specified 20 lots (fig. 4-13). These overly generous lots reflected a rural ideal that was entirely inappropriate in a rapidly growing city. In particular, the initial lots were far too big for standard urban types of the 19th century. As soon as the city began to be settled, the original lots were quickly subdivided, but not in any standard or modular pattern.

As a result, the tissue that survives today is almost entirely haphazard, despite the rigid structure of the original grid. Subdivision, combined with an unusual system of orienting lots in different directions on every other block, makes a large and unruly perimeter development that is quite unlike the more orderly development of U.S. grid cities (fig. 4-14). The disorder persists, particularly in the odd mix of types it has enabled: hospitals next to small houses, retail superstores flanked by tiny corner stores (figs. 4-15 and 4-16).

This disorder contrasts with the neighborhood just south of the original grid, which was the location of Salt Lake City's original outlots. Instead of according to a religious and rural ideal, the subdivision here occurred more pragmatically. The lots were matched to the prevalent building type: 1920s bungalow housing. The resulting neighborhood varies slightly from street to street and has no overall plan, but the consistently sized lots provide an orderly tissue that supports a strong and resilient place.

The lessons from Cincinnati and Salt Lake City clearly point to the importance of an original tissue plan in establishing and maintaining typological and morphological order. Where a plan is discordant—the building types that are in current demand do not match the pattern of land subdivision being provided—that discordance can be carried forward for generations. Where land subdivision, even in small organic increments, is created to support common building types, the neighborhood usually maintains its consistency over time through natural and spontaneous redevelopment that fits the underlying pattern.

Sadly, as in Cincinnati, aggregating land into a large site is one of the most popular interventions of modernist and even contemporary urban design and government policy. By assuming ownership of multiple tracts and tearing apart the existing fabric to create a large project, the owner or government may actually harm the ability of the city to heal itself incrementally

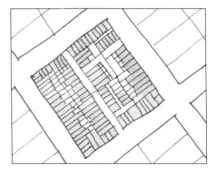

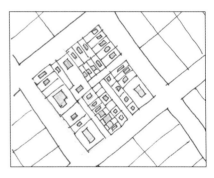

4-13 (top) | Brigham Young's ideal plan for Salt Lake City included lots of 1.3 acres and streets 132 feet wide, entirely inappropriate for the subsequent urban development. Note how the orientation of the lots shifts from block to block.

4-14 (middle) | A Salt Lake City urban block as it was actually built out using multiple haphazardly planned alleys and mid-block streets

4-15 (bottom) | A Salt Lake City block with medium density is even more haphazardly developed, with great variety in lot size and building type. Compare to the New York grid, at the same scale, in Figure 4-4, on page 49.

4-16 | *Salt Lake City's out-of-scale tissue enabled an odd mix of types and scales to develop over time. Here, small houses survive next to a one-story office building and a high-rise condo.*

through small organic changes. The large parcel may become a long-term problem, since it now requires a powerful or very resourceful entity to adapt it to new life when it comes time to do so.

ENDNOTES

1   Some call this process "organic," but I am reserving that term for a slightly different meaning.

2   Gianfranco Caniggia and Gian Luigi Maffei, *Interpreting Basic Building: Architectural Composition and Building Typology* (1979; Florence: Alinea Editrice, 2001), 130–34.

3   Peter Hall, *Cities of Tomorrow* (Oxford: Blackwell, 1988), 126–27.

4   One exception to this was when developer Ken Schnitzer, starting in 1967, assembled 127 acres for a mixed use development in Houston by purchasing more than 300 separate single-family homes.

5   Les Christie, "Die, Die, Monster Home! Die!" CNN Money, http://money.cnn.com, August 18, 2005.

6   Since 1980, almost half of the homes in West University Place, a Houston city, have been torn down and replaced with much larger houses.

7   Caniggia and Maffei, *Interpreting Basic Building*.

8   Brenda Scheer, "The Anatomy of Sprawl," *Places: A Forum of Environmental Design* 14, no. 2 (Fall 2001): 25–37.

9   Brenda Scheer and Daniel Ferdelman, "Destruction and Survival: The Story of Over-the-Rhine," *Urban Morphology* 5, no. 2 (2001): 15–27.

10   Aldo Rossi, *Architecture of the City*, trans. Diane Ghirardo and Joan Ockman (1966; Cambridge, Mass.: MIT Press, Oppositions Books, 1982).

CHAPTER 5: LEGITIMACY AND CONTROL

The idea of type described in the discussion on the suburban office building in Chapter 3 acknowledges the conditioning influences on the type coming from function, image, technology, market, and culture. My description of this type is specifically analytical, a way of understanding the form and its process of formation and transformation without interjecting idealism or judgment. One may not consider this building type ideal or even acceptable, but exemplars do exist in great numbers, and thus the type has affected metropolitan form quite profoundly.

But there is a certain aura of legitimacy contained in my analysis: The type is "true" in the sense that it honestly reflects the forces and conditions that form it. It is also true in the sense that it accurately reflects a very specific culture and a set of underlying values. I am asserting that as a culture, we have certain values and daily practices, and they in turn become the conditions that influence the type.

In contemporary suburban America, these values tend to glorify what might be termed *real estate functions*: The suburban office type is a commodity. Its market appeal, price, convenience, and profitability trump other aspects that could have been conditions that influence the type. Examples of these other kinds of values, which resonate with a certain subset of people, are: fit with the urban context, design and material quality, social equity, and sustainability.

In other eras and other places, types would not be described using a typology that glorifies the conditions of real estate value. The concept of type, however, usually carries with it the notion of judgment, legitimacy, or validation. With the suburban office building type, legitimacy is obtained by conformance with the values of the culture, which are specifically market driven. The type would not be legitimate if it did not work successfully in this way. Because these forces are strong, a planner who must evaluate either the type, or a specific example of it, has to deal with the real estate values that are driving it, not just the much less influential community values that he or she is advocating.

In the past, typologies have been developed that use different frameworks of validation; some examples include taste, social propriety, reflection of nature, adherence to classical forms, or functional and structural efficiency. For many centuries, iconography and fit with a divine cosmology were the key values. With the exception of functional and structural efficiency, these values have little bearing on the prosaic suburban office-building type, although they do have importance in contemporary culture in some places and with certain types.

One of the major ideas imputed to typology is that typologies confer legitimacy on architecture. However, not all typological systems are legitimate at any moment in time. Ultimately, typologies are measured against something that is reflected in the values of the culture of the era. The value of cultural continuity is embraced, for example, if an architect employs types that have historically been associated with a particular use: a cathedral or classical temple. Modernist architects rejected that value and expected architecture to be based on typologies that reflected a resolution of function and structure.

All buildings can be analyzed using any of these typological systems, but some are found wanting or degenerate because they do not rise to the level of legitimacy in that system. Whether or not a type or any exemplar is legitimate depends on what typology it is measured against: ideal form as developed in the crucible of culture, an ideal system, or ideal suitability.

In the current climate, and throughout the late 20th century, the Enlightenment ideas of typology discussed in Chapter 2 have been revived as a way of evaluating and legitimizing individual architectural designs and the form of the city itself. For the most part, individual projects or approved types are measured against a value we might call "the continuity of the city."[1] This value was revived in architectural circles beginning in the 1960s, as a response to modernism's willful rejection of the historic fabric of place.

Today, planners more and more frequently use type to claim that this or that project or scheme has validity—correctness—because it appears to be typologically consistent with traditional urban form, perhaps as exemplified in a nearby place. This is often what is meant by the terms *contextual design* and *compatible design*.

Urban continuity as expressed in typological and morphological continuity is the theoretical basis for the legitimacy of form-based codes and for some design guidelines. This is a substantial change in basis from earlier forms of regulation, which were guided by the modernist emphasis on functionalism, rationalism, and expressions of technological and economic progress. At the moment, planners and designers are caught in the inherent struggle between these two value systems.

Contextual demands, and form-based codes in particular, can be aggravating to some architects. Their concern is that most projects must legally fit an approved set of types in order to be legitimate—that is, evaluated as good or beautiful. Under this system, architects must contend with the stated or unstated judgment that good design is no more and no less than an elaboration on a limited set of precedents. Architects have been trained to value innovation and the expression of current cultural ideas in their work, not conformance to a type, however much freedom that type may allow. It is not surprising that they push back against restrictions such as this.

Many contemporary theorists believe that the attitude of innovation that has been drilled into architects has instigated a crisis in the urban environment that only attention to urban continuity can mend.[2] Many architects, on the other hand, are often less resistant to codes and seek ways to satisfy both urban continuity and innovation, willing to leave aside the most destructive antiurban modernist interpretations.

Urban continuity as a system of legitimacy is problematic beyond the issues of architecture, however. For one thing, urban continuity as an approach cannot, by definition, logically extend to the 20th-century disruptions to the continuity of urban form, specifically suburban types, nonurban types, and suburban form.[3] New urbanism views most building of the last 70 years as an aberration, an unfortunate blip in an otherwise stable continuum of urban construction for thousands of years. In this view, contemporary types and their configurations are sometimes rejected out of hand as unacceptable, despite their typological resilience and adherence to contemporary values. The new urbanist answer to the suburbs implies significant destruction and wholesale rebuilding of a huge proportion of the U.S. metropolitan landscape.

Even more difficult, however, is the value-system shift this implies. The purpose of the movement, aside from making more aesthetically pleasing places, is rooted in the desire to recover or to create more-livable places, where people enjoy walking to work, greeting their neighbors, supporting their local shopkeeper, and avoiding long commutes. Urban continuity, in short, is meant to support a completely different lifestyle from what most people are accustomed to. What is gained may be clear: a sense of community, a savings in energy and pollution, less land consumption, and a more enjoyable aesthetic overall, among many other things.

For now, despite these advantages, most people still adhere to values that support the narrow conditions that create and sustain the typologies of the suburbs: the prestige and privacy of big houses on big lots; the homogeneity and social life of neighbors; the freedom of cars and freeways; and the convenience, variety, and abundance of big box and mall shopping. As long as these values dominate the general culture, the very different urban and small-town values associated with urban typologies can only make inroads in relatively small enclaves.

These are not absolutes, of course. One can have a big house and two cars yet live close in and enjoy urban experiences and even take the bus once in a while. One can occasionally shop at Target and yet studiously patronize local merchants and farmers markets. A shift in values sometimes seems imminent, particularly if you are the type of person who walks the line between these value sets.

That line can be a difficult one for planners. Planners who are put in the position of interpreting between these differing value systems can face a storm of opposition from both camps. The perspective that needs to be maintained is to always be on the lookout for change, for the evolution of values and the evolution of types that portend a movement.

URBAN DESIGN, PLANNING, AND URBAN FORM

Accepting, for the moment, that current planning practice points in the direction of urban continuity and that sustainability goals are not incompatible with this practice, it is clear that planning controls that exploit an understanding of morphology and typology can be very successful in controlling the look and feel of a physical environment and its urban design.

By contrast, for much of the 20th century, planners operated with tools that were inadequate to address urban form; and indeed, that was not their intention. In the 18th and 19th centuries in the United States, cities and towns were invariably founded with a grid of streets. Over time, as a place grew, new town land was needed, and a new section of gridded streets was added to the first, sometimes with a slightly different orientation and a slightly different scale or block structure (fig. 5-1). Therefore, at the heart of most American cities is a set of gridded districts, now often interrupted by an overlay of highways, railroads, and utility corridors.

The grids of streets created blocks, and those blocks were subdivided to be sold off at the same time the grid was created. The lots thus created were scaled to receive specific building types. A variety of building types could be accommodated because grids and lots are not always uniform. A close examination of the historic lots and blocks in some places reveals a sophisticated understanding of this idea.

In New York City, for example, the lots that face numbered streets are relatively narrow and were intended for common housing types. When lots on the same block faced the wider avenues, dimensions shifted, and larger,

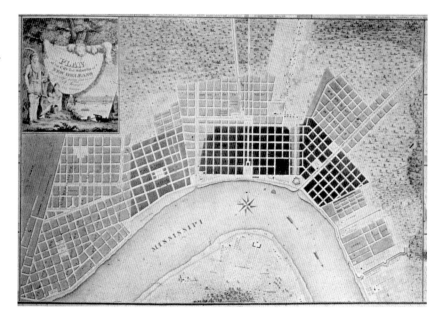

5-1 | New Orleans is a classic example of an original grid of streets with newer grids added over time, bent slightly to orient to the bend in the river (1817).

grander types were built. Some of these support commercial uses. (See Figure 4-4, p. 49.) Although much of what was built no longer exists, this contrast in scale and type persists today, with large grand buildings presiding over the avenues, while smaller buildings cluster along the streets.

Perhaps the finest example of this grid differentiation can be found in Savannah, Georgia, with its lovely parks and streets. The character and types found here vary because some streets are interrupted by parks, while others are not.[4] Alleys provide a third level of distinction (fig. 5-2).

Because these places were built with a common understanding of the building types, and with very real technological and material limitations, the initial development tended to be quite consistent. The lot dimensions, which were minimal to support the types, acted as a check on development, preventing intrusive and overscaled projects but also reinforcing a specific density.

This situation prevailed into the early 20th century, when zoning was first introduced. At the time these codes were developed, it was assumed that some kind of orderly tissue—a grid of streets and lots—would exist; so, for example, a 10-foot minimum setback would provide a consistent frontage and prevent a tone-deaf builder from invading the common space of the street. Design was already restricted, so to speak, by the consistent types and the lot and street dimensions.

The standard for the zoning laws of very large cities provided the legislative template for all places, no matter how inappropriate. Cities at the turn of the 20th century were overcrowded and unhealthy to a degree that is hard to imagine now except by visiting third-world countries. Responding to intense and persuasive urban issues of that age, the ideals reflected in zoning, especially in places such as Chicago and New York, addressed problems of intensive and very unhealthy overcrowding; noxious industries and their resulting smoke, toxins, and water pollution; and the lack of access to green open areas. The ideals conveyed in the zoning laws included, naturally, separation of land uses, provision of greater open space, and limits on the size and density of buildings. But since zoning's main purpose was to prevent noxious land uses, such as tanneries and other urban industries, from invading nice neighborhoods, the importance of the underlying tissue framework was never emphasized.

Since zoning emphasized land-use and intensity limitations, physical dimensional limitations were somewhat neglected, especially since zoning was promoted at the dawn of the automobile era, when urban dimensions, orderly blocks, and consistent types could be assumed. As development pushed out to the suburbs, this framework also disappeared. Without an orderly underlying tissue and consistent lot size, the few dimensional aspects of zoning, such as setbacks and floor area ratios, had no consistent physical results.

Transferring zoning ideals to small towns and suburbs never made much sense, but that transfer occurred anyway through the standardization of zoning codes throughout the country. The zoning template allowed even small towns some measure of control that had not existed, and they seized it in record numbers. The control of land use, in particular, was a very powerful

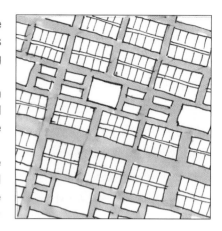

5-2 | A complex and fine-grained pattern of lots, blocks, and open spaces enables a variety of building types in the brilliant plan of Savannah, Georgia. Different street types are also implied in the plan. The sustained loveliness of the city is due to this plan and the spontaneous, orderly development it enables.

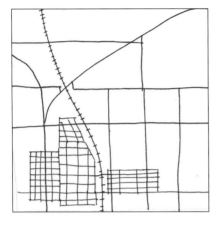

5-3 | *Initially, towns were founded with a continuous grid of streets, even if the grids varied as they were added.*

5-4 | *Later, foundation by grid was abandoned, and noncontinuous, independent subdivisions became the norm. Without a grid, access to the subdivisions was concentrated on a single road.*

tool that gave city leaders a politically attractive leverage over virtually all landowners. The politicization of zoning, and its usefulness in manipulating land values, made it an even less effective tool for formal control.

The early 20th century gave people the means and the incentive to move out of the city and into the countryside: the private automobile. The standard grid additions gave way to a wholly new kind of place development: the stand-alone subdivision, barely anchored to the old system of roads that connected towns (fig. 5-3).[5] Town founding and orderly growth through the means of a layout of grids and grid additions halted completely. Urban development exploded beyond the bounds of these limitations. A sparsely distributed set of country roads, instead of dense urban grids, provided the backbone of all urban development, which was sporadically extended into the countryside (fig. 5-4). Highway builders struggled to keep up, widening the former country roads over and over to accommodate the traffic.

A new set of controls was developed to overcome another set of problems with isolated subdivisions. Subdivision regulations were devised to set construction standards and minimum sizes for new lots, and these tended to match the goals of zoning: lower density, green spaces, and an enforced consistency of use and size. These standards were also technical, including the sizing and minimum specifications for sidewalks, lighting, grading, sewers, water, and the like. Because these were isolated places, the actual layout of the lots and streets did not receive much scrutiny, nor was continuity of the urban fabric acknowledged as a concern. As subdivisions became the only system of creating new local streets and lot patterns in expanding areas, jurisdictions gave over their historic town-planning role to private interests.

As long as the primary tools to control private development were so general, the urban design of places was impossible to control. Cities allocated land to different uses, but the uses could and did take an infinite variety of forms, so the results were both unsatisfying and physically unrelated to one another. Cities also laid out approximate locations for arterial streets and highways and dictated the amount of open space, but they did not plan their own street networks or arrange open space as a complement to public space design. Open spaces were relegated to leftover land.

The manner in which zoning has been applied has also been a failure for urban continuity. An older section of a town might have a consistent tissue and common types, but these have been ignored in order to apply the ideal zoning formulas that privilege large lots, open space, and large setbacks. Thus, a nice older neighborhood in Denver—where the average size of a lot is 4,500 square feet—until recently was zoned for a minimum lot size of 8,000 square feet. The lack of association between the reality on the ground and the zoning restrictions has caused much difficulty, especially as neighborhoods change and buildings turn over within them.

By the middle of the 20th century, it became fairly clear that zoning was not sufficient to control development, preserve great places, and actually plan for attractive growth. Two related planning ideas grew from this dissatisfaction: historic preservation and design guidelines. Preservation

focused on recognizing and saving places, especially individual buildings that retained their historic character. Many neighborhoods that might have been destroyed by the misguided application of zoning were saved by preservation efforts.

Design guidelines were inspired by the effectiveness of historic preservation efforts. Without much thought, jurisdictions based them on the template of historic preservation guidelines, emphasizing materials, details, styles, and sign controls. These were applied to nonhistorical neighborhoods in an attempt to control the aesthetic quality of places and manage change.[6]

Many issues arise in the application of design guidelines, whether regulatory or not. Most of these stem from the difficulty of defining "good" design and from the need to justify most regulations on some basis. Guidelines, often very arbitrary, are difficult to develop, are difficult to administer, and go against the grain of what most people feel is their right to determine how their property looks.

Perhaps the most important shortcoming is that design guidelines are often ineffective in producing a coherent urban environment, unless one already exists. Design guidelines tacitly promote the idea that the disorder and ugliness of the urban environment is a cosmetic problem, that it can be solved with sign controls, consistent styles, street trees, and a limited color palette. Without an understanding of the importance of morphology and typology in creating order, guidelines can have peculiar results. This happens when an arbitrary style is applied to a contemporary type, such as the pueblo-style strip shopping center or more banal examples of contemporary types dressed up with less than authentic historic styles (fig. 5-5).

TYPOLOGY AND CODES
Much of the task of urban design is to foster a sense of order in the built environment, while still allowing growth, change, and a great diversity of

5-5 | An example of a contemporary building type, a strip shopping center, built meticulously using details of the old pueblo style, 1993, Phoenix, Arizona. Most examples of this kind today employ a far more generic and banal imitation "historic" style.

5-6 | *Old town of Park City, Utah, with its messy signs, parking, color, awnings, activities, and detail overlaid on a very consistent static tissue and small variations on one or two types. The effect is lively yet orderly.*

activities, aesthetics, and forms. While order can be created using a variety of techniques—landscapes, vistas, axes, geometric configurations, and architectural consistency—our newly burgeoning value of urban continuity privileges a particular kind of incremental physical arrangement typified by lots, blocks, and open spaces arranged in traditional configurations.

Even this kind of order can actually be quite messy: The underlying tissue of the city grid of most big cities creates substantial orderliness, even though there is a cacophony of signs, uses, type variations, and the visual messiness of everyday comings and goings. This is a lively urban order. Having a strong tissue and similar building types creates a background datum against which a lively variety can play (fig. 5-6).

In this kind of environment, the order is found as a background, mostly provided by the uniformity and consistency of the tissues and a certain overall consistency in building types. The urban types themselves work best when their architectural language is within a range of scale, variation, and richness, defined by the rhythms of openings in the facade, three-dimensional depth, and material application, rather than style.

On the other end of the spectrum is the calm, leafy green order that we associate with suburban subdivisions and office parks. The underlying tissue here is just as orderly: a pattern of similar-sized lots and streets, with a related set of building types. Instead of the cacophony of lively and visually stimulating objects layered onto a strong order, we have "soft" order—widely spaced and somewhat varied types, with a gentle but steady rhythm of house, space, house. A variety of site conditions—lawns and driveways, walls and fences, gardens and groves—provide variety and visual interest (fig. 5-7).

These two environments represent two poles in the kinds of districts where attention to building types and tissues is an effective technique for controlling urban form. Their commonality is that they have an underlying

street and lot pattern—static tissue—that retains a basic order and provides a strict limitation on what can be built there. For example, in a typical single-family neighborhood, the lot size and orientation restrict the size and general type of the building. Circumscribing that further are legal restrictions such as setbacks and height limits. Uniformity is gained through these, while variety comes from variations in materials, colors, landscaping, details, and, to a lesser extent, some variation of the types found in the neighborhood.

In order to reinforce a sense of order and allow for variety in static districts, it is necessary to define and preserve the critical characteristics of the tissue and the common building types. This same strategy works whether you are talking about a suburban neighborhood, a business park, or a lively urban downtown. It is possible, and sometimes desirable, to manipulate the standard controls of traditional zoning for this purpose, although certain concepts such as floor area ratio, which has no predictable formal result, must be abandoned in favor of clear delineation of maximum (not minimum) setbacks and building envelopes.

Changing traditional zoning parameters in a given jurisdiction is often easier than substituting an entirely new and untried system of controls such as a form-based code. On the other hand, zoning regulations are very strict in their application of land-use separations, which may not be

5-7 | The rhythm of landscape, lots, and similarity in size bring order to a street where houses are widely varied types.

desirable in a more urban environment. And zoning is a useless tool for formal control if the underlying tissue is highly varied and there is no sense of typological consistency.

Even in consistent static tissues, zoning is a tool designed to direct land use and economic and functional priorities, not form. It may not be possible or appropriate to use zoning to address the subtleties of building types. A possible alternative is aesthetic zoning, or form-based codes, a system of regulation that explicitly foregrounds the formal characteristics of a place as the critical criterion to be controlled. Form-based codes usually discard zoning altogether and replace it with a place-based regulation of formal configurations that can be built, which implies a range of density and some limitation on land use. However, land uses are more lightly regulated so that a mix of uses in a particular district can be promoted. Form-based codes recognize different neighborhood configurations and densities, and they act to preserve and enhance the relationship between each property and its surrounding physical and formal context.

FORM-BASED CODES AND TYPOLOGY

Form-based codes are designed to preserve static neighborhoods and create new development that has specific formal layouts and goals. Such codes are specifically typological, in that they implicitly reference the types that are acceptable in a place, according to a set of ideals that usually give preference to higher-density development. Although types are referenced, they are not usually described holistically in a form-based code. Instead, they are described by regulating their pieces and parts: frontages (architectural features on the public way), setbacks, building envelopes, side yards, and so on.[7]

The code is developed and applied in different districts that correspond to different densities and appropriate types. As with zoning, there is a map, with delimited territories where different regulations apply. Within those boundaries, a form-based code will enumerate frontages, setbacks, lot sizes, building heights, parking, and land uses.[8] Building types can also be defined and restricted. In addition, there may be some regulation of the street design, with attention to sidewalks, travel lanes, and landscaping. Civic spaces can also be required and regulated as to their function, design, and location. Some form-based codes go further and regulate the building design—materials, window shapes, and so on. Form-based codes thus combine the functions of subdivision regulation, preservation, and design guidelines, and they hark back to the traditions of old-fashioned town planning.

Given this program of regulation, it is easy to see how the concepts and flexible logic of urban morphology and typology can be channeled for this purpose. As in lot-block and all other static tissues built in history, the expected and customary building types are the foundation that inspires the creation of a specific tissue pattern. A form-based code uses regulation to create or strengthen an urban tissue and to restrict types, whether by defining types or by defining a building envelope and other details. Form-based codes are a way of returning to a tradition of city building, albeit with heavy regulation instead of the limitations of expectations, culture, technology, and custom.

The underlying assumption of a form-based code is that the physical configuration of a place can be manipulated as a means to control economic function, density, social goals, and ecological priorities. Like zoning, however, and unlike traditional city formations, form-based codes have a very specific political and social agenda, so that they legitimize certain building types and disdain others. The ones that tend to be ignored or shuffled off into special zones are some of our most enduring and prosaic types: the suburban office building, strip shopping centers, gas stations, storage buildings, stadiums, big box stores, airports, and so on. These are types that do not tend to be compatible with the small-scale lot-block static tissue that is the key element of the effectiveness of form-based codes.

USING MORPHOLOGY AND TYPOLOGY IN FORM-BASED CODES

One of the shortcomings of form-based codes as they currently are promoted is that they are not usually place specific. The SmartCode used in many places as a template specifies eight categories of place—known as transects—with very specific regulations and types appropriate for those categories. It also suggests calibrating the code to common local types, which is usually interpreted as adopting some of the unique building types or frontages found in a place.

If codes are really to be reflective of place, however, common templates must be rethought entirely. Creating a code requires that an existing place be thoroughly analyzed for its morphological history and its current typological conditions. The subtleties of the tissue formation and evolution are particularly revealing of why and how a place developed over time, and what the forces still acting on it might be. For example, it would be important to understand Salt Lake City's peculiar grid and its effects over time (see Chapter 4) to prepare a code that would respond to those unique and still extant conditions. Superficial analysis and application of a standard transect would miss the importance of lot size and orientation to the subsequent failures in the urban context. Opportunities to exploit the large block size and unusual alley structure would also be lost.

Form-based codes on undeveloped land require the development of an underlying tissue, which must be exactly specified by the planner or the developer. The code will not operate correctly without a plan of the tissue, which is analogous to the old grid plan layouts used by town founders everywhere.[9] Sophisticated variations within the lot configurations of the plan, especially those responding to natural conditions, street variation, and civic space, could suggest a variety of acceptable types, as they do in Savannah, Georgia.

In the historic process of town development, tissues were designed to fit the types that were common at the time of the tissue formation, not to make a statement about density, best practices, or the like. A key lesson, drawn from Salt Lake City and other places, is that creating a tissue that is misaligned with common development types can have repercussions through time. Idealism, whether it is Brigham Young's ideal low-density village or the new urbanist ideal high-density village, will only go so far in holding back the forces of urban development and transformation.

As a start for a form-based code, the acceptable types should be drawn from regional examples, with the idea that building types are regionally unique and created to address specific conditions. In some places, duplexes are common; in others, they barely exist. The theory of typology assumes that there are economic, social, and environmental conditions that shape demand for types. Designing a place for an unproven type or one that clearly is not really desired will slow down the development and cause other problems later. The tissue plan and the code developed for new areas of a region should recognize common types or encourage slight modifications to common types that already exist in that region.

Where a pattern already exists, it should be thoroughly understood, particularly the forces that have acted on it. Only then can a code be aligned with the typological transformations that have already occurred and will likely occur in the future.

A particular issue is the proposed reuse of some older types, for example, a row house. Some historic types are no longer viable due to modern building codes, technological innovations, and car culture. Their modern equivalents may not have the same character or public face.

FORM-BASED CODES—A CAUTION

Although form-based codes are a way of creating and enforcing order, they cannot be used for certain kinds of existing tissues. As we have seen, the concepts of type, morphology, and the fit of a certain tissue to the common types are very relevant to creating a form-based code. But without a clear and relatively small-scale static tissue, a form-based code has little meaning, just as a given zoning setback has no physical result on a five-acre site.

Therefore, form-based codes are a reasonable solution where static tissues occur, yet they have very limited applicability in regulating the elastic or campus tissues that dominate in the suburbs. (See Chapter 4.) Where a consistent tissue does not exist or cannot be created with new development or by repair, the problem of creating order and variety is much more complex and cannot be simply guided through a hands-off application of form-based codes. (See Chapter 6.)

Several other critiques of form-based codes can also be asserted, based on lessons that typological transformation and morphology present to us. The first is that ideology can be a problem. The Enlightenment concept of type was born in a crucible of ideology, defining as good those buildings that reflected the ideal types, based on their origins and their evolution from classical forms. Quickly, though, that idealism gave way to the judgment of types based on their fit with function, standardized classical parts, and structure.

The return to idealism today is troubling. Typological transformations always move away from their historic origins, by branching into several different new types or by extensive modification. These types respond to exact values and conditions at first, and then become common and stubbornly persistent standards, before finally being supplanted by new types. To the extent that form-based codes recreate anachronistic places or require anachronistic types, they are moving against the tide of evolutionary development and have a risk of failing.

There is nothing in the technique or regulatory methods of form-based codes that requires a backward-looking agenda, however. But, just as with the initial applications of zoning law, there is a desire to codify a set of ideal formulas and principles that address perceived problems in present-day American cities. These problems are chiefly centered on auto-centric development and sprawl, and the answer seems to be higher density and a mix of uses.

In the 1920s, zoning took aim at deplorable overcrowding, pollution, and the lack of open space. Yet we are still living with the techniques of zoning, even though the problem set has completely changed. Adaptation of the zoning technique to new problems has been difficult, not because the tool lacks flexibility but because of the initial idealism attached to zoning and thoroughly encoded in it. Zoning encourages the public and their officials to view urban problems as questions of general density, land-use separation, and street hierarchies.

The technique of form-based coding is not limited to solving one or two contemporary issues—it might be flexible enough to solve different kinds of problems as they arise in this century. This will be true if certain idealistic agendas are not so firmly attached to the technique and are replaced with a more pragmatic and open-ended position. A variety of goals should be offered, with examples of how coding can be applied. Form-based codes could be effective in problems of environmental degradation or landscape integration, for example, but not if the "right" answer is always higher density, pedestrian districts, and mixed use.

The key to this kind of flexibility is to recognize urban change and transformation as central conditions of all active cities. In a form-based code, this will mean abandoning inflexible ideals or standardized formulas in favor of representing and codifying the actual place as it has been acted upon over time. Even new development occurs in the regional landscape and reflects the farm roads and fields that were its residents' first marks on the land.[10]

Successful and truly urban places change constantly, especially at the level that design guidelines were created to control: signs, colors, and porch details. Enacting a code that freezes current types might seem attractive to those who fear change, but it will limit the ability of types to have transformative effects and successful adaptations. Looking back at Over-the-Rhine or any 19th-century city, it is clear that a dense fabric arose on the same tissue template of smaller types. Historically, it would have been unfortunate if there had been a regulatory resistance to replacing the poor wooden structures with grand five-story buildings.

On the other hand, the emphasis on creating sound tissues in form-based codes is completely consistent with the desire for orderly change: The initial urban tissue has immense effect on the future development of the city. It may not be the only way to organize an orderly place, but it is a method that offers enormous flexibility for the future.

For this reason, form-based codes should be explicitly about guiding change, not preserving a place as a historic relic. New types will eventually evolve and replace the types put in place today. How can the form-based codes created today allow and encourage this eventuality while still providing order? It may be possible to design form-based codes to be minimally restrictive, as opposed to the current trend that planners have in mind to regulate all things physical. A strong emphasis on carefully designed and varied tissues and public spaces is the most obvious answer, a lesson we can easily glean from a place such as Savannah, Georgia. By the same token, building types should be defined with more flexibility, and design guidelines should be very limited, in order to insure that types can evolve and respond to changing conditions and tastes.

ENDNOTES

1   Anthony Vidler, "The Third Typology," *Oppositions* 7 (Winter 1976): 3–4. Vidler suggests that the city itself is the current measure of legitimacy—the "third typology," following earlier typologies of, first, nature and, second, function as the basis for evaluation.

2   See the works of Gianfranco Caniggia, Attilio Petruccioli, and Douglas Kelbaugh.

3   Attilio Petruccioli, "Exoteric, Polytheistic, Fundamentalist Typology," in *Typological Process and Design Theory* (Cambridge, Mass.: Aga Khan Program for Islamic Architecture, 1998), 9.

4   Stanford Anderson, "Savannah and the Issue of Precedent: City Plan as Resource," in *Settlements in the Americas: Cross-cultural Perspectives*, ed. Ralph Bennett (Cranbury, N.J.: Associated University Press, 1993), 114–37.

5   Michael Southworth and Peter Owens, "The Evolving Metropolis: Studies of Community, Neighborhood, and Street Form at the Urban Edge," *Journal of the American Planning Association* 59, no. 3 (Summer 1993): 271–87.

6   Brenda Scheer, "Invitation to Debate," in *Design Review: Challenging Aesthetic Control*, ed. Brenda Case Scheer and Wolfgang F. E. Preiser (New York: Chapman and Hall, 1994), 1–10.

7   See SmartCode, created by Duany Plater–Zyberk & Company, available as open source online at www.smartcodecentral.org/smartfilesv9_2.html.

8   D. Parolek, K. Parolek, and P. Crawford, *Form-Based Codes* (Hoboken, N.J.: John Wiley and Sons, 2008).

9   Practitioners developing form-based codes use the term regulating plan to refer to the entire map of a place that identifies areas subject to different regulations, which would be analogous to a zoning map. This is not the historic meaning of the term. Some also refer to each specific area as a transect—analogous to a zoning district—another confusing use of the term, which also has a different meaning in history.

10 Brenda Scheer, "The Anatomy of Sprawl," *Places: A Forum of Environmental Design* 14, no. 2 (Fall 2001): 25–37.

CHAPTER 6: TYPOLOGY AND THE DISORDERED CITY

Within a static tissue, even substantial variations in types and transformations in scale can seem comfortable and can be managed by planners with relative ease. But the last 50 years of urban development have seen the rapid build out of many areas that are much more disordered. Knowledge of typological and morphological conditions that guide change in these areas is even more critical, but it is much more difficult for planners to manage.

As we turn our eyes away from the block-ordered city or drive out of the orderly subdivision, we encounter an urban order that did not exist before the advent of the car culture. Drive along any arterial road and the pattern is much the same: big box stores, drive-through restaurants, strip shopping centers, small office buildings, and, of course, acres of parking (fig. 6-1).

The building types that line the arterial are as standardized as any in history. Like all building types, they are the result of an evolving set of conditions and values that have shaped their configurations minutely. Planning ideals and planning theory cannot alter the existence of these types since they are not arbitrary constructions but finely tuned instruments of the economic and cultural forces that caused them to be built (fig. 6-2).

So it is with some doubt that I look on "before and after" visualizations of such an area, showing parking miraculously gone, buildings moved up to the street, and roadbeds narrowed with trees, sidewalks, and transit.[1] Of course, this representation is done to illustrate to people how much more pleasant and friendly the place would be if these changes were accomplished. It is impossible to argue with this conclusion, based on the vision portrayed (fig. 6-3).

Unfortunately, transformation of the urban environment is much trickier than creation of a Photoshop rendering. A simple analysis of the problem of the highway strip reveals some of the difficulties:

Types such as big box stores and large single-purpose stores—for example, Petsmart—are linked to global distribution systems. As they have evolved, their economies of scale are such that they cannot exist as smaller stores in smaller shopping districts that serve smaller market areas. They require large parking and loading areas. Because of this scale and the traffic it generates, they are not pleasant to live close to or even to connect to with pedestrian

6-1 | Colerain Avenue in Cincinnati, is an example of elastic tissue. Note the disorder of buildings and wide variety of lot size, shape, and orientation that face the arterial street.

6-2 | *Suburban arterial types include big box stores, strip shopping centers, freestanding restaurants, warehouses, car lots, and low-scale office buildings, as shown in St. George, Utah.*

paths. As these types are currently conceived, they are not amenable to a mix of uses. These types are extremely resistant to change in the short term, since our values lean more toward low-cost shopping and large-scale convenience than to community interaction and walking to shop.

The arterial road that serves these areas, unlike the old urban grid, is usually the single through road for the immediate district. It must carry a huge amount of traffic. The arterial street is the backbone of a hierarchy of roads that we take for granted but that is fundamentally different from the streets of traditional cities, which were all joined together in a connected, much less hierarchical system that provided multiple paths of travel (fig. 6-4). Here, there are no interconnected alternative streets and no outlet from traffic congestion. All the subdivision roads empty exclusively onto the arterial, making it the only access for most residents. For most of the day, it is a very large river of cars and trucks that is completely unsuitable to pedestrians. Over time, it has been widened to the point that it is uncomfortable for any human-scale activity.

The underlying ownership patterns—that is, the lot patterns—along the arterial are deeply disordered. Since a lot is basically the unit of change for any area, one or two properties that can be brought into conformance with a plan may have little effect on the remaining lots. Unlike static areas, these properties have no necessary relationship to one another. Without a static pattern of lots to restrict them, building types vary widely in size, orientation, and configuration.

Finally, the arterial, with its continuous pattern of loose development, runs for miles and miles, like a long, linear city, fronting on acres and acres of very low density housing that is itself static. While it may be possible, especially with transit stops, to provide enough density and a mix of uses to transform one or two intersections along this endless linearity, it taxes the imagination to understand how an entire corridor might be transformed.

6-3 | Before and after images of an arterial proposal

But the goal is surely to transform such areas. They are ugly, not sustainable, dependent on the car culture and its burning of fossil fuels, and frighteningly ineffective at supporting a wide variety of urban social interactions, especially for children and the elderly. The very unsuitability of such places has inspired designers and planners to imagine the alternatives demonstrated in the "before and after" renderings.

If we study actual places rather than ideal ones, there are a few instances where a stretch of arterial has been transformed over time. One such location is Wilshire Boulevard in Los Angeles, where the real estate demand has provided a narrow band of linear high-rise development in what

6-4 | *A wide arterial road in Arlington, Texas, is typical of the scale in many suburban places.*

was once a low-scale environment. But Wilshire Boulevard was never the entirely disordered strip that we find in our suburbs. It started its life with a long downtown pattern, which aided its eventual redevelopment. Peachtree Street in Atlanta has a similar history.

There are plenty of interesting ideas about transformation. Most involve providing higher-density development at specific nodes. Many other ideas involve making these environments look better and more comfortable by transforming parking areas with landscaping, signs, and potential for multiuse. The former approaches favor ideals and do not address the inexorable challenge of strong existing typologies. The latter bring landscaping and signs into a semblance of order to make places look better, but they usually do not affect the inherent lack of support for social interaction or sustainability.

IMAGE AND TYPE

The typologies that dominate the strip seem very durable and inevitable, and they are as finely tuned to cultural and economic conditions as the *insula* type that preceded them. On the other hand, they have arisen and flourished under an extremely specific set of conditions, almost a hothouse environment, which is demonstrably not as enduring or culturally adaptable as conditions that determined the *insula* type. Not only do these types respond to these specific conditions—global distribution, car culture, low land cost, land ownership patterns, consumer preference, and arterial supremacy—they are also completely dependent on this specific and delicate mix of conditions. If any of these conditions change, the entire pattern of these types could be toppled, and the types could rapidly transform or become obsolete.

We already know that on a 20- or 30-year time scale, arterial strips are relatively unstable.[2] They are subject to greater change than other kinds of tissues—frequent land-use changes, new buildings, reconfigured parking, and so on. These changes and shifting conditions are both subtle and interesting to watch. The evolution of some types, especially those associated with very specific businesses, such as fast food, has been formidably rapid.

While all this change is happening, very few planners or designers are paying much attention to the nature of it. One thesis of this book is that such changes actually portend real transformation and that studying them is like studying the evolution of an organism in real time; it helps us figure out what might realistically happen next and what can be done to encourage useful transformation and discourage or even outlaw bad ideas.

For example, one suburban trend is the *fake type*—buildings that appear to be one type but are in fact a wholly new type. Nonfunctional decoration merely gives them the appearance of an earlier type. For instance, in suburban shopping centers planners sometimes require storefront types that look like the old *insulae*, with a store on the ground floor and some other use on the second floor. The storefront exists, but the rooms on the second floor are seldom occupied, or they may not exist at all—they are just an illusion (fig. 6-5). This is not a market-driven requirement, but one based solely on the desire for a more urban appearance.

Some fake types adhere only partially to the physical character of the original type, or they are a marriage of a fake type and a real type. There are many examples of strip shopping centers—a genuine type—dolled up with the appearance of a two-story building and unique store facades. This gives them the appearance of another type: the old-fashioned village main street, albeit with a design that bespeaks all-at-once, rather than accumulated. Even big box stores are being designed with facades that have the old-timey look of multiple independent stores (fig. 6-6).

Even without the urging of planners, developers have embraced fake types in much greater numbers recently due to a characteristic of building types: It conveys a strong message of association with the past, whether a building is a contemporary rendition of a type or a fake. A sophisticated architect will often repurpose a historic type in order to call attention to ironic or political ideas or to convey a subtle message. The real estate and planning sectors use fake types to invoke an overt themed image: the small-town Main Street. Rather than being ironic or subtle, this use of type is pure marketing and branding. The image of a small-town, accumulated street—which embodies ideas of home, local business, neighborliness, small scale, long-term associations, and control by individual local people—is repurposed to support a large-scale strip shopping center with chain stores. The old-fashioned small-town attributes and values are belied by the fast turnover, large market areas, corporate control, and rapid churning of start up chains in the strip shopping center.

Make no mistake, this is not an evolution of the type since the type remains fundamentally the same: a strip of undemised commercial space leased to different businesses in blocks, serviced at the rear, with a parking lot out front and a continuous sidewalk to serve all the stores. It is fundamentally the same, because the conditions it responds to are the same conditions that made it successful in the first place. Now it is clad in a different architectural style. This is the difference between theme—or image—and

6-5 | *An example of a strip shopping center with a fake second floor, in Phoenix, Arizona*

type. The image invokes a different type than the building actually is, but the building still performs as a strip shopping center and everyone who uses it has expectations that it will operate as a strip shopping center, not as a series of old-time Main Street shops.

SEEKING ANSWERS IN TYPE

Still, the rapid adoption of the fake type is a positive sign of our desire for a different kind of environment that offers a sense of comfort and addresses social and community values that have been trampled in the development of

6-6 | *This Walmart has been designed and massed to mimic a smaller-scale multi-store shopping street.*

the global–automotive–suburban real estate jumble. Rather than attempting to make buildings look like something that they are not, however, the lessons of typology indicate another path. Because building types evolve, it is possible to closely observe changes and trends in the actual environment and to support changing conditions that are already tending to move the type or its urban arrangement in a more desirable direction.

This incrementalist attitude is quite different from applying an idealistic model, but it might be more effective. Ideal models, while they look possible and delightful on paper, can be impossible leaps to implement except under very strong market conditions coupled with heavy-handed restrictions and laws.

Take the current vogue of suggesting the transformation of the arterial with buildings that line the street, as in an old-fashioned downtown. These proposals imagine *insulae* types built at the lot line, with parking in the rear. Yet it is like swimming upstream to propose an *insulae* type for arterial development: The type is not suited to the conditions of most suburban commercial development. Contemporary six-lane arterials have little in common with the small-scale streets required to support this type. The failure of this type can easily be predicted based on these conditions alone; and the reluctance of developers to risk failure means that legislating the *insulae* type will tend to stop development and redevelopment, rather than to move it in a forward direction. The more that the type is seen to fail, the less likely it will be that it will be used in another location.

Some big box chains are beginning to offer smaller store-model options to communities that insist on them, but this is a trend upheld only by regulation, not by other conditions. Small Wal-Marts, unless they are more cost-effective, will never be the natural choice of that corporation.

On the other hand, there are some far more promising ideas that are actually happening on the ground without much input from planners. In other words, we can observe typological evolution in response to conditions that are changing in the culture. We can also predict other changes, and any change to the conditions that support suburban arterial types will have a very rapid impact on those types, due to their elastic nature, their extreme dependency on a few factors, and their very short general endurance as buildings. For example, if the nature of automobiles changed—say, we all started driving much smaller electric vehicles—our urban areas would not be greatly affected, but the suburban arterial strip would change rapidly in response.

ONE ALTERNATIVE FUTURE

One of the long-term evolutions that can easily be observed in many arterial strips is the tendency to have a double layer of businesses: Pads are located on the front edge of a property housing small types such as freestanding stores or restaurants, while larger types—big box and strip shopping centers—occupy the back edge of the property, farthest away from the street. A large parking area is sandwiched between these two layers. In an

6-7 | *An unusual retail center in Salt Lake City has buildings that back up to the arterial and surround a small-scale parking court.*

area in Salt Lake City, the site plan has been deftly altered to take advantage and adapt accordingly. Here, the front is occupied by a natural-foods grocery store, but it is oriented toward the center, away from the arterial, so that the back of the store is on the street edge. The sides of the lot, which is on a corner, have also been developed facing the interior parking lot. On the back of the lot, away from the arterial, the types are slightly more urban, with two stories of development and smaller footprint buildings. Adjacent to this interior parking, also in the back, a small suburban office building has been built. A short walking path, adjoining a similarly planned shopping center, connects it to a residence hotel. Apartment housing is planned behind this. A natural stream runs between the two properties (fig. 6-7).

This example uses all the well-known and common types, but they are arranged in ways that subtly reflect the current trends, with slightly more density and a much more urban appearance. The result is an interestingly scaled interior parking area that acts as a forecourt or plaza to all the development. When a sidewalk market animated the edge of this parking lot, it was easy to see how it might be transformed into public space from time to time, or even permanently, were certain transformations to occur that reduce the amount of space needed for cars (fig. 6-8).

One can imagine that a series of these parking courts along an arterial might eventually provide a relatively dense and deep development pattern that does not rely on the arterial itself for pedestrian life (figs. 6-9 and 6-10). If cars become much smaller and lighter or communal, these courts might become the backbone of a series of landscaped public spaces. This projection also takes into account the current depth of the property and its potential and actual relationship to the housing near it.

6-8 | *In this retail center in Salt Lake City, Whole Foods takes over part of the parking lot for a Saturday festival.*

Out on the arterial street, there is another innovation, no doubt a result of ambitious public planning rather than an evolutionary trend. The back end of the big box store in Figure 6-10, with no entrances, was carefully designed with landscaping and architectural detailing rather than a blank wall (fig. 6-11). It even boasts an elevated dining deck overlooking the busy street, which is landscaped.

This lively shopping area is quite popular and worthy of imitation. The advantage to imitating this strategy is that it is based on observation of the market and social conditions, rather than a set of abstract ideals. It acknowledges certain key truths: The parking lot is the space of human interaction for places like this, not the uncomfortably scaled arterial street; individual property owners would like to maximize the retail and rental space by using double depth, which frequently exists already; arterial roads with high traffic are not particularly pleasant or safe places for people; and slightly changed existing types are the most ubiquitous and reliable patterns of development and are therefore the most expeditious to be built.

This is only one example, and its success depends on the specific conditions of the place. The parking court idea will not be viable where the frontage property is not deep enough for a double layer of development, for example. Other workable ideas can also be gathered from close observation and analysis of the transformations already going on, among them the transformation of former big box types, which are often obsolete because they are no longer big enough.[3]

This example demonstrates several conditions that are changing, though, as suburbs continue to build out. These include a new interest in architectural detail in retail commercial spaces (the old-time Main Street image is also an example of this); the acceptability of a reduced parking ratio; the lack of need to advertise a large parking lot in order to attract consumers; and the desire for better design overall, especially of the visible back of the big box store. This project also has a small amount of structured parking, made possible and necessary by a rise in property values. That parking is mostly used by employees and office workers. The smaller amount of parking helps maintain the interesting scale of the parking court.

Some of the key design concepts found in this project are:

1. Buildings all face the parking court, creating visible pedestrian activity.
2. Building types and scale are the common single-use types for suburban development, but a mix of uses is found around the parking court, not in any single building.
3. Curb cuts are extremely limited on the arterial, and loading is artfully handled.
4. The parking court dimensions and the scale of the facades that overlook it are carefully planned and detailed.
5. There are clear and attractive connections to adjacent properties along the arterial, minimizing the need to go back out onto the busy street just to go to the next shopping plaza.

6-9 | Before: A typical plan of a wide arterial with big box stores fronted by smaller buildings

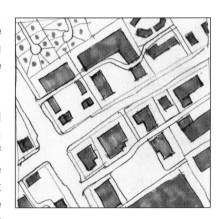

6-10 | After: Parking courts and more buildings or uses added to the same plan, creating a more intimate internal circulation and open space away from the arterial

6-11 | *The rear of the Whole Foods store that faces the arterial features landscaping, a well-designed facade, and a raised area for outdoor dining. The entrance to the store is on the opposite facade, oriented to the internal parking court.*

6. The project takes advantage of a streamlined walkway threading into the neighborhood, to connect the space of the parking court to residential properties.
7. Parking ratios are minimized. Some parking is on the roof or incorporated in structures.
8. The street wall on the arterial is strong and well designed, although it has no openings.

PLACES OF COMPLEXITY: MASTER PLANNED AND SINGLE-OWNER DEVELOPMENTS

In contemporary practice, an aggregated parcel is much more valuable than smaller pieces, which cannot be developed as readily with the enormous-scale commercial types we think of as *master planned*. These campus tissues are often embedded within districts where static tissues dominate—for example, a shopping mall surrounded by residential subdivisions. Recently, campus tissues have been seen as opportunities for redevelopment of master planned, mixed use villages that are like islands of isolated urbanism.[4]

The three tissue types identified in Chapter 4 are: *static* tissues; *elastic* tissues, the roadside arterial patterns discussed above; and *campus* tissues. A campus tissue is characterized as a single large parcel of land under single ownership or control. Most campus sites contain a number of buildings and some internal car access or private streets. Within any city, many such places can be found, often related to public or institutional ownership; examples include universities, airports, medical centers, civic centers, prisons, and high schools. Private campuses are also common: shopping malls, factories and industrial parks, golf courses and other recreation, warehouse and storage, train yards, and large apartment complexes. Lately, some mixed use centers have been created on campus sites, and some have been redeveloped on the larger parcels of older uses such as shopping malls.

In the center of cities, campuses are much rarer, and they are relatively much smaller. The nature of urban development in the past 50 years has made these kinds of places much more common in outlying areas. For many planners, aggregation of property to create a developable large campus has been considered a positive goal of redevelopment. This is driven, in part, by development typologies that require much larger sites than may commonly be available in an older part of town.

In a morphological sense, these areas, no matter what their use, act as discontinuous islands in the urban fabric. The main urban design characteristic is the owner, planner, and designer's strong ability to control the design and use of every building and public space that is built on the property, versus a much weaker ability to control building decisions on property in split ownership. Property configuration is a key operating boundary for different urban design strategies: Without significant control, it is difficult to anticipate and plan for change.[5]

Campus sites invite complexity to evolve. Medical centers, airports, and universities, especially in dense areas, accrete buildings over time and thereby create problems of access, visibility, and orientation that are not found in lot-block static tissues or even in the elastic tissues, both of which always have clear public circulation (fig. 6-12). Designing and planning these complex places has become a subfield of its own. Building complexes such as this are difficult to manage as a planner, both inside and outside the institution, since they are driven by internal logic rather than urban conditions or patterns. The churning of buildings within a campus environment is remarkable, too. Without external constraints, changes are rapid and constant.

For a city planner, dealing with a university campus, an airport, a large apartment complex, or an army base can be a frustrating experience. They are like cities within cities—but without the basic morphological structures and with a tendency to wall themselves off from the immediate context. Control of the large parcel and the exemptions that large public institutions obtain from normal regulation mean these campus areas are like fiefdoms, where development can be either haphazard and neglected, or controlled with an iron hand by a single entity.

On the other hand, the campus tissue would seem to offer many potential answers to the dissatisfaction with current urban configurations of the outlying suburbs, especially where large parcels can be redeveloped. A mixed use planned development has the design potential of "big architecture": It can be designed as a physically and functionally intertwined group of buildings, integrated with parking garages and furnished with attractive public spaces. A single large property can be made relatively dense compared to the surrounding suburban fabric, and it can potentially restore connections to that fabric through the integration of streets and sidewalks.

But there are important questions that arise in the redevelopment of

6-12 | *A medical campus accretes buildings over time and may have little sense of access, visibility, and orientation.*

mixed use projects on large sites. For one, there is no internal logic set by normal building types in a campus plan, unlike the logic of a tissue plan with static tissues and common types. Building types within the campus tissue are extremely complex—for example, residential buildings adjoining or overlapping a shopping street, or office buildings atop parking garages, which extend over the boundaries of the adjacent land uses because there are no property lines to delimit separate buildings. The complexity of buildings in some new mixed use developments is just as complicated, unlimited, and intertwined as the most complex airport or hospital array.

This complexity is not an issue for the first few years of a development's life, but as time passes and conditions shift, complexity becomes the enemy of incremental or easy change. It is always true that the more complex and use-specific a building is, the less adaptable it is to changing conditions.[6] The simplest buildings, divided in increments of small ownership—such as single-family houses or *insulae* in older cities—have nearly infinite adaptability due to their building configuration, and it does not take enormous capital to alter them. This model is exactly the opposite of what is found in the large-scale mixed use developments now being built, even though they are often designed to mimic the appearance of a diverse and small-scale urban fabric.

The complexity of the campus tissue challenges the ideal of incremental transformation that is assumed as part of the urban continuity paradigm. As with modernist urban renewal projects, these places are built all at once, according to the latest ideas. Some new urbanists are critical of the entire suburban landscape and promote this kind of sweeping redevelopment. This is a somewhat ironic condition since our current ideals of urban continuity derive from our dissatisfaction with the large-scale modern 20th-century car-culture form. The all-encompassing modernist forms themselves were created in reaction to the teeming unhealthiness of dense urban form in the 19th century. Intense reactionary swings and the subsequent wholesale destruction of what has come before should give us greater pause.

We do not yet know what the collateral damage of sweeping away a century of accumulated typologically evolved urban fabric might be. We can only solve the problems currently presented to us and use our insights from the past to avoid making mistakes. It is our curse that we scarcely remember the reasons why modern, clean high-rise towers were promoted and why acres of old urban fabric were demolished to make way for them. Perhaps the most important lesson is this: Huge change is risky. Given the choice, it might always be better to subdivide rather than to aggregate, to choose incremental adaptations over the wholesale and monumental do-overs that are required for the large-scale mixed use project.

It is easy to see that a single-built campus of urbanity is a very different construct than a piece of a city. It mimics only the look, not any of the other urban qualities or conditions that provide the resilience of naturally evolved places and types. Those qualities include regular and divided lot patterns, public streets, relatively simple building types situated individually on lots, and multiple connections to surrounding fabrics.

ENDNOTES

1   See, for example, the work of Steve Price, www.urban-advantage.com.

2   Brenda Scheer, "The Radial Street as a Timeline: A Study of the Transformation of Elastic Tissues," in *Suburban Form, an International Perspective*, ed. Kiril Stanilov and Brenda Scheer (London: Routledge, 2003), 102–22.

3   E. Dunham-Jones and J. Williams, Retrofitting Suburbia (Hoboken, N.J.: John Wiley and Sons, 2009), 66–69.

4   Ibid. Dunham-Jones and Williams have documented many examples in their thorough review of the topic.

5   N. J. Habraken, *Palladio's Children: Essays on Everyday Environment and the Architect* (Oxford: Taylor and Francis, 2005), 77.

6   Ibid., 105–10.

CHAPTER 7: TYPE IN DESIGN AND PRACTICE

As we have seen, types originally arose as a way of legitimizing specific patterns and qualities of a building, a way of labeling some buildings acceptable while finding others not so. Historically, types were seen as culturally influenced, formal ideals to be used as inspiration but to be manipulated for specific places, conditions, and uses. Identifying an abstract form as an ideal—the common example used is a round temple—did not limit any particular exemplar except to the extent that it needed to carry the bare minimum of common formal identifiers: a dome, a colonnade, and of course, the barrel shape.[1] Designers were free to vary the proportions, column design, orders, and, to a limited extent, the materials and size. In the Enlightenment, when formal typological ideas originated, classical styles were the only forms accepted for this kind of manipulation, and only the grander examples were treated to this validation.

The power of type, exemplified by this concept and carried through to today, is that types provide designers with a boundary—a common vocabulary, customary relationships, even materials and modes of expression—while allowing any particular exemplar to be a modified example of the type. Modifications were accepted for scale, site, cultural specificity, and particularly for function, which changed dramatically throughout the 18th and 19th centuries with the industrial revolution. Although modernists rejected the specificity of classical types, they nevertheless adopted a similar mode of thinking that encouraged limitations on formal configurations, structural systems, and material expression. In both the Enlightenment neoclassical version and the more austere modernist version, the referent was essentially autonomous: Types were endowed with, and architecture was judged against, a preferred set of aesthetics. Although explained as natural or based on function, structure, or production, the judgment of correctness actually owed as much to the "correct" aesthetic as passed down or reinvented and repurposed—for example, as machine imagery was repurposed.

In the mid-20th century, an expanded idea of type arose because of dissatisfaction with the limitations imposed by these typologies—in particular, the modernist's lack of responsiveness and even rejection of the historic city fabric. Flipping the idea on its head, architects in the mid-20th century revived and altered the idea of type so that the historic types evident in the city—rather than classical ideals—became fodder for a new or evolved architecture. In order to complete this operation, detailed investigations of the city and its architecture were necessary.[2] These investigations were opened up so that it was no longer solely ideal monumental types that were studied but also ordinary buildings and the ordinary fabric—streets and lots—that constituted the bulk of the city and lent it much of its character. Further exploration established that these ordinary historic urban places were not designed or modeled on exemplary or ideal types, as such, but owed their particular form to a kind of unconscious evolution and accumulation over time.

Thus was born the second understanding of type: types as *expressions of cultural values*, arising from suitability and fit to circumstantially evolved external conditions. Ordinary types as exemplified in the historic city are not refined abstract ideals but are the resultant of basic relationships of form, circulation, lived functions, prestige, economy, and other cultural priorities. Unlike ideal types, they are not consciously *refined* over time; instead, they *evolve* over time without regard to refinement or any other conscious attempt at progressive improvement. Thus, typological transformation will occur most frequently in response to external, culturally determined changes of the society and not through the consciously developed ideals of architecture, unless they somehow coincide.

Type as *ideal* and type as a *resultant of culture* are two very different ideas. Although conceptually the division between these two ideas of type is clear, it is not realistic to maintain. It is obvious that there are nondeterminant ideals and rules embedded in even the most prosaic conventional types, such that ideals "pollute" the full responsiveness of any type.

In sharp contrast to those working in the classical and Enlightenment eras, when types were defined as ideals, designers today are far more likely to use type for the design of ordinary buildings rather than monumental ones. Unlike architects in historical eras, architects today do not usually look to formal types as exemplars for unique buildings such as concert halls, museums, and grand cathedrals, except to provide a particular reference or analogue.[3] "My new airport recalls the train station's grand hall," they might say. Architectural design encompasses a freer and more explicitly creative arena for these special buildings, which by contemporary convention are expected to be unique and not to conform overtly to a recognized type. As unique expressions, these special buildings also do not evolve as formal types the way that more-ordinary buildings do.

But for many prosaic buildings designed by architects, and for virtually all buildings where a designer is not involved, the method of design today starts with building type as a jumping-off point. Donald Schon has performed a number of studies that follow designers as they puzzle through design problems.[4] He has determined that building types are a critical shorthand in the thinking of almost all architects, whether they call them that or not.

Probably the most common way architects use a type is as a template or model that needs only elaboration, adjustment for the site, and specificity of materials, details, scale, and so on. This is especially true when the formal type and use-type are closely aligned, as in the example of the suburban office building in Chapter 3. To begin the design of a building is to consciously explore the known form-type, perhaps adopting it spontaneously. If given the assignment of designing a freestanding garage, to take a simple example, the designer first accepts the common type and then considers adaptations that are appropriate.

Beginning with the standard type means that there is no need to derive the basic form from first principles, no need to invent the large doors, the boxy shape, the single story, the dimensions required for each car. Adaptations flow easily after the initial type is engaged—more storage, a room above, an interesting material combination. These adaptations are layered on top of the initial concept of the type that exists in the imagination of the designer, a priori. That conception, that idea of a specific type, is drawn from the experience of the designer: her observations and informal categorizations of a series of preexisting examples with common formal characteristics.

This method of adopting a type as a template is very common for the vast majority of buildings in the urban and suburban environments. In our culture, it is not practical to create an original and unique form for each shopping center, office building, and gas station. Moreover, even if unique forms were proposed, they would be untested in terms of their match for the function, economy, and image of the use, so they would be at risk of failing in ways that a known type is not.

More-complicated buildings can seldom be designed using a single type as a template. Thus, it is almost as common for a designer to combine two or more formal types, usually by simple juxtaposition. An example might be a recreation-center design that conjoins a double-loaded corridor type with a gymnasium (fig. 7-1). Each part has typological characteristics, but the location or quality of their juxtaposition is not predetermined by either type. Since the combination of types is not as deterministic as the single-type template, the relationship to use is far more variable. This particular combination could easily be used for a school or a small church, for example, or any use that has certain characteristics such as the need for a large high-ceilinged space and a part with much smaller rooms. By using slight variations of the two basic alternatives that are juxtaposed, the designer can infinitely adjust the diagram of a building. What is still assumed, though, is the typological integrity of each piece: circulation of the double-loaded corridor, its array of rooms opening up on each side, and the windows on the exterior of the "classrooms." These bespeak a very common experience, and certain expectations of what will happen there and how people will perform in it.

By adding the site and urban context to the diagrams—the drop-off, the parking, and delivery—the problem becomes more constrained, so

7-1 | *This diagram of a building juxtaposes two different common building types: a classroom wing and a large high-ceilinged space.*

that the entrance location is probably narrowed down to a few choices. The shorthand of the type combination helps resolve the diagram. Schon has found that experienced designers can cycle quickly through the choices and winnow them according to a wide variety of individual criteria derived from experience and intent.[5] Architects may also *adapt* a type for a given situation. The situation may vary from the solution set solved by the type in several standard ways: It may vary in size, site, cultural meaning, the standard functions, material concerns, efficiency, specific codes, or climate.

There are far more subtle ways of using type as a mental construct in the design of a building. For example, a designer may choose some but not all aspects of a type—the entrance portico, for example. Alternatively, the designer may recognize overall similarities between the design problem and the problems solved by a known form-type. The designer may begin by temporarily adopting that type as a mental experiment—subsequently rejecting it or transforming it—even if the type at first glance (for instance, a train station) has little relationship to the problem (a stadium).

In any of these methods, the designer probably uses the type as an *authority* to a greater or lesser extent. Using the type of the suburban office building as a template, for example, the designer can appeal to its very commonality and successful repetition to justify his design as correct. The current type is so sensitively tuned to the market, site, and cultural function that it makes sense to adhere to the type closely and only design its particulars: selecting the facade materials and articulation, the signs, the shape, the site orientation, the elevator cab, and so on. There are still an infinite number of design choices, but they are constrained by the logic of the type.

In any of these instances, a designer might quote from aspects of one type or another type in order to invoke a characteristic of the type that is contained in our collective memory of it. Experts disagree on the degree to which architecture is able to convey specific meaning by such formal means. It is more reasonable to think of a building type as being able to convey an emotional or physical response—a sense of enclosure, heightened grandeur, cozy familiarity, and so on. In the example of the *insula* type, we have already noted that it conveys a subtext of small-scale community interaction, even when it is co-opted for globally based commerce.

Architects may also reject a particular type, as a person might do if designing a garage or an office building. This is often an artistic decision, rather than a rational response to the type pattern. Rejecting the common type is a way of exploring the culture, technology, or function for the purpose of invention, art, expression, and meaning. Rejection of the standard type is, on some level, unexpected or jarring. It might convey an intentionally subversive or critical message—using a type associated with palaces to house a corporate headquarters is strong commentary. At the very least, rejecting a common type in favor of something else conveys a message that the building will be unusual. Types might also be rejected because the situation or conditions are so radically different from what the type dictates; a good example of this is a difficult or especially spectacular site.

CLASSIFYING CONTEMPORARY TYPES

For planners working on form-based codes or other aesthetically driven regulation, the analysis and classification of types may be a key step to regulating change in an existing area. For designers, precise definitions of specific classifications are probably less important. Most architectural type studies begin with dividing the universe of buildings into use-types, such as libraries, schools, and clinics. In the definition of type used in this book, function has been de-emphasized in order to emphasize the important role that form itself plays in how a particular building operates within the urban and metropolitan context. This is consistent with typology's great 20th- and 21st-century role in analyzing and improving the way we build and design cities and suburbs.

There is no established classification of building types, owing probably to the immense variety of types all over the world and their slight alterations over time and in different places. Nomenclature of types suffers from the same sort of irregularity, so that in order to actually refer to a specific type, one must not only name it but also define most of its typological characteristics. There is also a problem of resolution: How precise does the definition of a type need to be?

Although there are potentially many completely unique classification systems that would distinguish one formal type from another, in support of the continuity of the city paradigm, the one proposed here is based on the relationship of types to the city. It is looking first at the site conditions, then the basic diagram of a family of types, then the potential parameters that distinguish actual types from one another. Within the final category, function is a condition that can contribute strongly to the physical characteristics that determine type, but it is not a physical characteristic itself. Figure 7-2 is a diagrammatic outline of this classification system.

FIRST LEVEL OF CLASSIFICATION:
THE URBAN CONTEXT

Building types are highly dependent on the site and the particularities of the lot. In contemporary practice, the universe of all buildings can be first divided into two site categories, which can be labeled *joined* or *freestanding* (figs. 7-3 and 7-4). These two can also correspond to what we think of as *urban* and *suburban*, although their location is not part of their determination. All building types fall into one or the other classification.

A *joined* building is one that is built to a property line with the intention of having another building on the adjoining lot. When fully built out, the buildings create a continuous fabric even though the underlying lots are in separate ownership, the buildings can be distinguished from one another, and they are highly varied in size, type, and style. Examples include the *insula* type

7-2 | *A classification system for types that begins with site distinctions and diagrams of basic shape.*

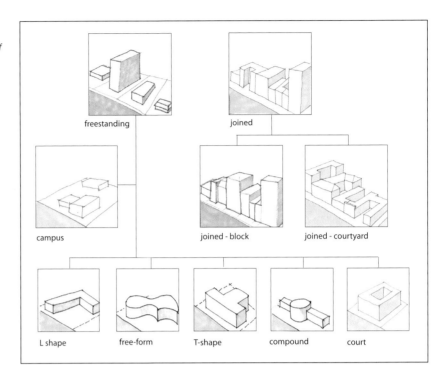

and row-house type, which were common for centuries. These types and other joined types formed the urban fabric of all dense cities and towns until the 20th century.

Over time, joined types will form a continuous urban fabric, with the distinguishing characteristic of an underlying lot system that regulates the development of the fabric. Each lot cannot be very much larger than the footprint of the building, so there is a necessary agreement between the building type intended or ultimately designed for the lot, and the size and shape of the lot (fig. 7-5).

There are common varieties of these types. The first variation has to do with the location of the site. If a site occupies the corner or the end of a row, the type is likely to be modified. In joined types, standard shapes are abstracted as rectangular, whereas the lots that the type occupies can be oddly shaped quadrangles or even multisided lots. In these cases, the exemplar of the type must be modified to fit the site, since the type stretches to fill the lot to the party wall.

Freestanding buildings are those buildings that occupy their lots so that there is unbuilt space surrounding them on all sides. Single-family houses, big box stores, and gas stations all fall into this classification (fig. 7-6). Historically, freestanding types were common in the country and in villages but were unusual in built-up cities. In urban places, a freestanding building was a luxury that frequently denoted some special use: a cathedral, palace, or civic building.

The freestanding classification applies to many highly varied building

Clockwise from top left: 7-3 | The joined site configuration. 7-4 | The freestanding site configuration. 7-5 | A city fabric of joined buildings shows the variety of sizes and site conditions possible. 7-6 | A city fabric of freestanding buildings. 7-7 | A city fabric showing a variety of campus configurations. Note that the buildings within each campus are freestanding.

types encompassing every use from stadium to drive-up photo booth. The most prolific example is the single-family house, which itself has many variations that can also be termed separate types. The heterogeneity of freestanding buildings makes distinguishing different building types very challenging. To make matters even more complicated, there are many instances of freestanding buildings that do not seem to conform to a single type; they are examples of hybrid types or are no discernible type at all. This is a rare occurrence in joined urban buildings, which demonstrate much less diversity of form.

The relative lack of formal constraint in freestanding buildings is one of the issues that confound us when we analyze the suburban environment. In urban buildings, the limited site and the need to create party walls dictates a limited repertoire and a correspondingly greater emphasis on the articulation of the building's facade and architecture. In suburban contexts—where the lot is much larger relative to the building—the orientation, scale, and shape of the building are not driven by the lot but by other conditions. This is less true for lots that are smaller and more uniform, as lots in many subdivisions are. These were often intended for uniform-scaled houses with very specific relationships to the lots.

In addition to having a single freestanding building on a lot, another significant variation on this classification is a *campus*, or a group of buildings situated on a single lot, under one ownership (fig. 7-7). Typologically, the buildings situated on a campus are almost invariably freestanding, but their relationship to other buildings is not defined by underlying lots and access to streets. One characteristic giveaway of the nature of this variant is that you may not immediately know where the "front" of any building is.

There are even more complicated hybrids: master planned developments. These variants do not arise in the usual evolved morphology of a place and may include both joined buildings and freestanding ones.

The second level of classification is the basic diagram of the building. Joined and freestanding buildings each have their own set of diagrams, which may look similar but are really quite distinct in the way they respond to different conditions. The diagrams of a freestanding building are highly varied, as we have noted. Figure 7-8 offers a few examples based on the following characteristics: the orientation of the building to the street, the number of stories, the relationship of the building to the lot, and the basic configuration of the circulation. None of these diagrams is a building type in and of itself; they are all highly abstracted shapes of a basic form or a hybrid

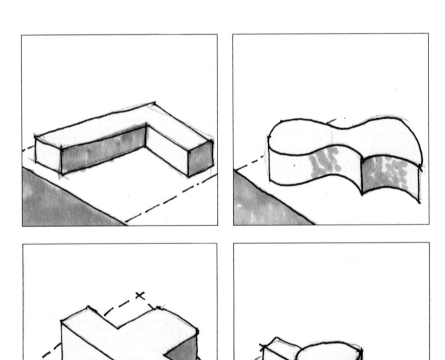

7-8 | *A few of the many possible freestanding building diagrams*

of two or more of these forms. Imagine that any of them could be very large (for example, a stadium) or very small (a house).

Within the classification of joined types there are two basic diagrams: a courtyard and a block. The courtyard building has at least one internal open space or is joined to other buildings that create an internal open space (fig. 7-9). Entrances to this building can be on the street or on the courtyard. The block building has its main entrance on the street and does not form an internal open space.

The final level of classification is the individual type itself, arising from one of the diagrams and a number of other common characteristics.

Distinguishing one type from another is an art, not a science. Whether or not a building is a different type from another similar type is often a judgment call based on the purpose of the type classification. Furthermore, there is no general agreement on the distinctions between one type and another or on how they are named or identified. Any particular analysis of any urban area will generate many arguments about whether a particular building is one type or another type, or no type at all. Sometimes it is not important to have a high level of refinement that distinguishes a type's resolution. Different classifications with different degrees of resolution can legitimately be proposed without damaging the idea of type in the least.

Any shorthand description of building types will always contain some notion of function. Having already distinguished urban/site and diagram, function now becomes a central and perhaps defining component. However, similar functions may be contained in very different types, and similar types can have or can evolve many different functions, which tends to prove how tricky the concept of function really is in determining form.

Type has been defined here as an abstraction of a series of buildings that share common formal characteristics. Most common formal characteristics are derived from global, or generalized, functions: These include internal and external circulation patterns, scale, relationship to site, spatial quality, openings, structure, and sometimes, specific building parts—balconies, for example—that are critical to distinguishing one type from another.

In determining the characteristics of a particular type, there should be two important considerations: (1) Which parameters define the type minimally? and (2) What is the level of specificity or resolution that might call for even greater definition? Returning to the *insula* type for a moment, we can see that the minimal definition of the type is its urban context and basic shape, and beyond that, its large-scale storefront openings on the ground floor and the presence of upper floors with smaller openings, internal circulation, and small rooms, usually used as housing (fig. 7-10). But other architectural attributes are found in almost all examples: a cornice line, a change of materials from the ground floor to the top floor, an articulated lintel dividing the upper floor from the lower floor, very lightweight materials and glass inside the storefront openings, and punched windows on the upper floors that are aligned vertically with the center line of the storefront openings (as in fig. 7-11). Could these properly be part of the definition of the type, so

7-9 | Joined buildings have two basic diagrams: block and courtyard.

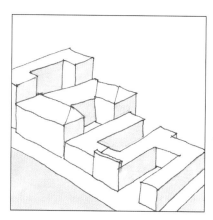

7-10 | An insula *type in Fort Worth, Texas*

that a building without these attributes would be excluded from the type?

In the French Quarter, in New Orleans, this same type has an even more distinctive variation: continuous wrought-iron balconies on the upper floors, with full-length door-windows (fig. 7-12). Is the French Quarter *insula* a completely different type because it has balconies?

A closer look at the French Quarter will demonstrate that what sometimes appears to be a standard *insula* building from the street is in fact based on a different diagram and thus a very different type: a courtyard building. In other cases in the French Quarter, the standard *insula* type has a unique adaptation: full doors on the upper level that open onto balconies. These two examples demonstrate the difficulty in determining whether a building is a particular type and also raise the question of why this level of specificity might matter.

The following examples compare different types that either have a similar shape, function, or look, so that we can more clearly see how a unique type is identified.

SHAPE AND MASS VERSUS TYPE

One of the diagrammatic varieties of a freestanding building is a long building with openings on one side and circulation along the same side, sometimes arranged in an L shape. This analysis takes two examples of this

7-11 | *An* insula *type in Brockport, New York. Are the changes of material from street to upper floor, the cornice line, and the punched windows characteristics of the type?*

7-12 | *The French Quarter, New Orleans*

diagram to demonstrate how other characteristics play into the definition of a unique type.

The diagrams of a strip shopping mall and a small motel may both follow this model, but there are substantial distinctions that make it clear that these buildings are different types and therefore warrant different consideration in planning and design.

7-13a-b | A single-story motel with an L-shaped, freestanding diagram, and a strip shopping center with the same diagram

While these two building types have two different functions, function is not a physical characteristic but a complex statement of the interaction of economics, people, and culture in a place. Functions often inspire or shape the physical characteristics of a type, but they are neither determinant nor complete. This is a subtle distinction, but it allows us to focus on the physical characteristics as the resolution of many kinds of forces related to operating, occupying, maintaining, and affording a building. These might include a particular real estate formula that is profitable, the very specific function of a motel, the tenants' cultural expectations of particular features, the need for privacy, parking and other site conditions, and the zoning and planning laws.

These conditions move the expression of the motel type in a different direction from the strip shopping type. To contrast, the motel type has fixed demising walls, a lighter structure with more internal supports, and an internal arrangement that takes into account public versus private expectations (fig. 7-13a).

In contrast, the shopping center has high ceilings, variable demising walls, a more solid structure with longer spans or bays, back entrances (but no windows), large storefront openings, a highly public front, and a private

7-14 | *Wheat Row, Washington, D.C., an* *example of a Georgian row house*

rear containing the office and storeroom. The orientation of the building invariably faces the open-ended part of the street, and parking is always located in a visible location up front (fig. 7-13b).

These characteristics are the defining qualities that differentiate types with similar diagrams: structure, entrance conditions, organization of internal space, relationship to parking and street, openings, and arcades.

GEORGIAN TOWN HOUSE VERSUS GEORGIAN HOME

Next is a comparison of two types that have a similar style and similar function. Both are single-family houses and have architectural features that can be called Georgian. One is adjoined—a row house, or what the British might call a terrace house. The other is freestanding—in the United States, it is known as a single-family house, while others might call it a town house. These different names are a small indication of the local variation and independence in naming types (figs. 7-14 and 7-15).

These two types have some things in common, but they actually diverge in type quite clearly because of their distinction in urban/site condition. The functions of the buildings are quite similar, although their internal arrangement

7-15 | James C. Daniel House, Wilkes County, Georgia, an example of a freestanding Georgian house

is distinct. In the row house, the rooms are arranged to take advantage of natural light at the front or rear of the house. In the single-family house, rooms open up to all sides. The location of windows and light drives the location of the circulation inside both buildings. Because of the relative narrowness of the row house, the door and circulation system are located on one side of the house, adjoining the party wall. In the single-family house type shown in Figure 7-15, the door and circulation are located in the center so that the rooms on the perimeter have light.

Using the parameters defined above, these two buildings are typologically distinct, not because of function but in spite of it. They do not share a diagram, structural similarity, entrance conditions, organization of internal space, relationship to the street and lot, or openings.

However, from some perspectives, these two buildings share a similar look and invoke a similar sensibility: graciousness, timelessness, wealth, and solidity. This look is a result of the particular style of the building with a flat brick front, large divided windows, a distinct cornice, contrasting trim, and a well-defined entrance.

This comparison demonstrates that similar styles can be applied to many different types, but it raises the question of the relationship of architectural style, materials, and details to type. Most of the time, the particular stylistic details do not affect the typological parameters, but that is not always the case: A colonnade is a good example of a parameter that can be both stylistic and typological.

SINGLE-FAMILY HOUSES

The single-family house has many variants of shape and type (fig. 7-16). Usually, a single-family house is a single structure on a single lot with open space all around, making it a freestanding classification. Two important

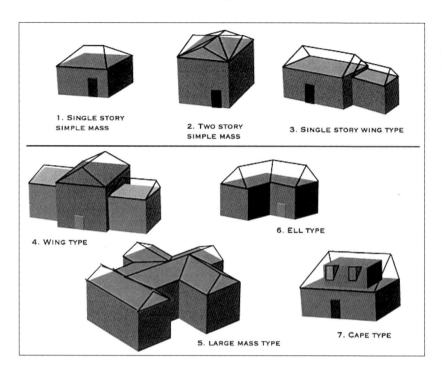

subvariants are topological: The courtyard house has an interior space, and the solid house does not. In systematically identifying single-family house types, the following are parameters that distinguish them, in rough order of importance:

1. A detached garage or one joined to the main structure, so the building is either a simple freestanding structure or a compound (i.e. attached) one.
2. Basic shape, including variations on roof, location of entrance, main structure and wings, and other major parts. This is often an indicator of the internal arrangement of the rooms and circulation.
3. Orientation of the house on the site, especially in regard to the street: In older houses, a rectangle is often oriented with its short side to the street. In newer houses with larger lots, the opposite is generally true. Other orientation conditions are driveways, distance to the street, side lots, relationship to other houses on the street, and whether the house is on a cul-de-sac, a curve, or a straight section of street.
4. Number of stories, the height of the building, and relative scale to other structures. Similar types can have great variation in scale.
5. Arrangement, scale, and shape of windows and other openings.
6. Porches, porticos, and colonnades, stoops and stairs, and other entrance markers.
7. Other formal distinguishing marks, such as towers or widow's walks.

Commonly, one would not consider the stylistic variations of a single-family house to have much importance in determining type. This is especially true of houses built in the United States after 1960, when style details were applied like so much chocolate or vanilla frosting on a limited number of types. For example, you can have a Queen Anne ranch house or a Tudor one. In earlier decades and centuries, the stylistic character went hand in hand with the type itself, making style and type more difficult to distinguish. The "Spanish" New Orleans courtyard house is an example of this convergence.

ENDNOTES

1   Giulio Carlo Argan, "On the Typology of Architecture," *Architectural Design* 33, no. 12 (1963): 564–65.

2   Nicola Marzot, "The Study of Urban Form in Italy," *Urban Morphology* 6, no. 2 (2002): 59–73.

3   Peter Rowe, *Design Thinking* (Cambridge, Mass.: MIT Press, 1987). Rowe examines multiple methods and theories designers use, mostly in the context of complicated design projects.

4   Donald A. Schon, "Designing: Rules, Types, Worlds," *Design Studies* 9, no. 3 (July 1988): 181–90.

5   Ibid., 185.

CHAPTER 8: TRANSFORMATION AND IMAGINATION

> If there is to be a new urbanism, it will not be based on the twin fantasies of order and omnipotence; it will be the staging of uncertainty; it will no longer be concerned with the arrangement of more or less permanent objects but with the irrigation of territories with potential; it will no longer aim for stable configurations but for the creation of enabling fields that accommodate processes that refuse to be crystallized into definitive form; it will no longer be about meticulous definition, the imposition of limits, but about expanding notions, denying boundaries, not about separating and identifying entities, but about discovering unnameable hybrids; it will no longer be obsessed with the city but with the manipulation of infrastructure for endless intensifications and diversifications, shortcuts and redistributions—the invention of psychological space.
>
> —Rem Koolhaas[1]

There are neighborhoods in most American cities where large 100-year-old houses persist. Often, these have been divided up for apartments or reused for commercial businesses. They have been added to or changed in ways that can be very similar: two-car garages that replaced carriage houses or barns, new large kitchens, multiple bathrooms, backyard amenities such as decks and patios, and technical upgrades such as air-conditioning and central heat. How and why did this transformation occur? Not only is answering this question within our reach, but doing so is essential to understanding what might happen to our own white-elephant single-family housing in the future.[2]

Can we not imagine our contemporary single-family houses 50 or 100 years hence? What technical changes, social reordering, and changes in transport and economic conditions are likely to remake the large-lot subdivision? Their very newness causes hesitation: Can we even imagine a transformation similar to the one we see every day in older neighborhoods? And if we can, what direction would we like it to go, and how can we shape it?

Imagine how a single-family neighborhood of 2010 might be transformed by 2110.[3] If we assume a low-energy household and some tension between the dense urban city and suburbs, garages and yards might be transformed to support high-efficiency mini-farms and cottage businesses and self-sufficient energy generation. Occupants might have fluid family formations, involving mostly adults. The stacking of electric cars would allow the streets to be narrowed but preserve the freedom of personal transportation.

Almost as important in this imagined future is what is *not* changed: the street pattern, separate lots housing one structure, and even the basic single-family housing type itself. This lesson comes from the study of the transformation of many older neighborhoods: Even after 100 years, we are unlikely to tear houses down, aggregate the properties, and start over. The persistence of these patterns is upheld by laws, property rights, infrastructure costs, and strong traditions dating back centuries. Even if we could tear it all down and start over—as modernists sometimes succeeded in doing—our collective record at successful rebuilding on a large scale is dismal.

Because these patterns persist in a consistent way in different places, we can study the past to help us understand and shape the transformation of the future. The study of type and urban form constitutes a way for individual planners and designers to develop a connoisseurship of the city—a finely tuned knowledge base acquired from deep observation and comparison of many places over time. These observations and more formal analytical techniques can lead to a fine grained understanding of the processes of urbanization and urban transformation.

Our current understanding of urban design frequently neglects these natural evolutionary processes of urban places, in favor of more formulaic solutions applied in a way that ignores historic patterns if they conflict with the ideals. The success of new urbanism has been a two-edged sword: On the one hand, the movement has brought great public awareness of the potential value of denser urban places, both existing and newly created. On the other hand, there have been far too many watercolor renderings of the same low-scale pedestrian town centers, with the same outdoor cafés; the same quasi-historic types; the same multicultural, multiage joggers on identical trails. The generic solution is not only trite and tiresome, it is also nearly impossible to build in most existing places, for which we can be somewhat thankful.

To be fair, the canon of new urbanism gives great respect to understanding existing urban places; it is planning practitioners who demand easy-to-apply formulas. On the other hand, some leaders of the new urbanists have been promoting the transect, a lazy person's guide to formulaic regulation that ignores specificity, on-the-ground conditions, and historic form and types.

Cities prior to the 20th century grew in continuous patterns of small additions. These formations were then left to evolve in more or less natural ways that not only resolved short-term conflicts but also accumulated working types that could themselves be altered in response to changing conditions. The terrible urban crises of the late 19th and early 20th centuries overwhelmed that paradigm dramatically, with the result that direct and swift intervention in the natural evolution seemed not only appropriate but required.

The 20th century saw the rise of two grandiose urban design concepts that require an outright rejection of evolutionary processes in the city. The immediate comparison between modernist city planning and new urbanism may seem ludicrous, given their different origins and goals, but they spring from the same kind of impatience with the slow-moving evolutionary processes of urban transformation. Modernist city design has been much reviled, but I would argue that some of the same attitudes and prejudices are also present in new urbanism. In both, there are formulaic, internationalized proposals that require sweeping change and destruction of large pieces of the existing city. Modernism reformed the old city; new urbanism looks to reform the suburbs. Both assume dramatic shifts in social values that are not yet evident. They both purport to solve immediate problems of the city: for modernism, disease, overcrowding, and pollution; for new urbanism, isolated forms, lack of public space, and sprawl. Most striking, both spawn a specific look—ideal urban forms and architectural expression. In each, the architectural formula is the most compelling branding of the movement, and in each, it has been easily distilled, commodified, and ultimately degraded by appropriation for banal economic goals that have little to do with the ideals of the movements themselves.

If not with ideal urban models, then, how else should we frame our urban design challenges? The study of the actual evolution of the physical city suggests many transformative mechanisms, transformations that can spark our imagination.

A different idea of urban design, one that returns to older processes rather than older forms, could be more effective. By conditioning ourselves to accept *what is* as the major frame of the urban field, we can *project* and plan the future from lessons and patterns of the past. *Projective urbanism* regards the urban field, especially the physical environment, as a resultant, or even a resolution, of cultural, technological, and historical conditions. There are as many different resolutions as there are places, so places are inherently unique. The conditions that form places are fluid. In projective urbanism, uncovering the immediate and historic conditions that have formed a place is paramount to understanding it well enough to plan for it.

Projective refers to the idea that future conditions and dramatic influences can be mapped or projected onto the existing urban field, using imaginative and intuitive processes and representations. The projections anticipate new technologies, for example, and changing social and economic values and priorities, but they also take into account the relative stability of various urban typologies and tissue formations. It is typological evolution and the natural constraints of urban morphology that stubbornly persist against idealistic formulas. As long as certain urban structures—static and elastic tissues—are in place and certain typologies—for example, suburban office buildings—remain evolutionarily sound, they will mightily constrain any sweeping changes.

PROJECTIVE URBANISM

Projective urbanism privileges existing and unique generative conditions, authentic cultural processes, incremental transformation, and physical pattern recognition. It anticipates technological, cultural, and economic changes and imagines their impact on unique urban places. It anticipates performance by users and subsequent typological transformation. It uses the understanding of historic typological processes to predict what is likely and unlikely under most conditions. It calls for designers to create informed and imaginative scenarios and to plan and to reiterate and modify those plans as new information appears or as the plans themselves begin to affect the environment.

This is analogous to planting a garden: Planting occurs after we gain an understanding of the nature of plants and the conditions for their growth; and then it is a constant effort of observing, adding, dividing, shaping, anticipating effects, and weeding. Most important, projective urbanism recognizes that the existing physical environment results from a complex history and culture, that rebuilding it—or even weeding it slightly—cannot be accomplished without understanding its natural growth tendencies and history and tapping into the cultural changes that are already happening.

Projective urbanism is not born out of theory or idealism. Rather, it is responsive to and engaged with the performance of contemporary people, altered by evolving conditions and processes and not singular and self-contained but allowing a potential flow of multiple programs and emergent ideas.[4] Rather than being a style or form, it is a method of analyzing places, reading their potential, and preparing the way for change to take place. Projective urbanism does not reject the existing suburbs or any form of urban development that is an authentic result of social, economic, historic, technological, and cultural conditions. Instead, it accepts the current place and its conditions as the field of play.

Importantly, projective urbanism does not require or promote particular styles of urbanism or particular urban forms or architectures, such as compact villages or isolated high-rise towers. (This deprives it of a branded image, but this also prevents corruption of the image.) Nor does projective urbanism reject particular solutions: It is open to the capturing and shaping of new types, to the evolution of new forms, to the deployment of new strategies, and particularly to the reshaping of emergent forms and processes.

Many smart growth regional scenario planning projects can be considered projective, although most are not very bold in their scenarios, assuming very few changes to technology or social structure. This is not very realistic for a 30-year projection, especially when we look back at the changes to the conditions that have influenced the urban environment over the *past* 30 years: the global economy and its effects on chain businesses, corporations, and distribution of manufacturing; women in the workforce; the entire computer and communication revolution; and the sudden criticality of global warming.

Projective urbanism might look to radically changing ideas of family composition, work habits, health technology, pollution standards, retirement, reduced population, leisure and exercise, new transportation options (shared cars or stack cars would have an enormous effect on some urban configurations), and, of course, energy conservation and generation. Although the ultimate results of these are difficult to predict precisely, it is unreasonable to neglect the effects of changes that are clearly already under way in the culture.

PLANNING FOR DIFFERENTIAL CHANGE

Urban planners need to fully understand that some of these changes will not affect the urban field, because many parts of the physical urban environment are impervious to change unless through radical and purposeful intervention. The urban tissue as a formation is relatively stable. The pattern of lots and blocks, once laid down, is stubbornly resistant to change, even after hundreds of years. Individual buildings and some building types, however, change on a fairly rapid time scale: 50 to 100 years.

The diagram in Figure 8-1 arises from research into historic urban change.[5] It ranks the relative stability of certain urban forms, versus the relative instability of others. At the bottom of the diagram is the land formation, or site, which is the most persistent and difficult form to manipulate. At the top of the diagram are the objects—signs, paving, street trees, fences—that people put up and tear down almost at will. In between are the buildings, tissues, and major urban structures that also persist in different time scales. These are urban structures that coexist in a place but are likely to change at very different rates, on time scales ranging from thousands of years to just a few days.

It is axiomatic that disturbance in any structure that normally is stable will catastrophically affect the structures above it that rely on its stability. Obviously, a great landslide that changes the site will destroy or alter the structures at the location. Less obviously, dramatic changes to the lots and blocks will likely require the destruction of the buildings and objects. For this reason, it is not reasonable to ignore existing property lines and streets when creating a plan, even in an undeveloped area.

What this diagram also suggests is that the most likely changes in the existing urban configuration are those on the layers of objects and buildings. Conversely, more attention must be paid to the items on the long-term time scales as new places are constructed. This implies that, because they are likely to shape development for a very long time, site development, open space preservation, infrastructure, and tissue patterns are far more critical than architecture, street trees, and even design guidelines.

IMAGINATION

The reason to study building types and urban transformation is to understand physical change, to predict change, and to shape change. History is a great

8-1 | *This diagram of the persistence of physical structures in the city shows a hierarchy from the most persistent forms (the site) to the most rapidly changing ones (the objects).*

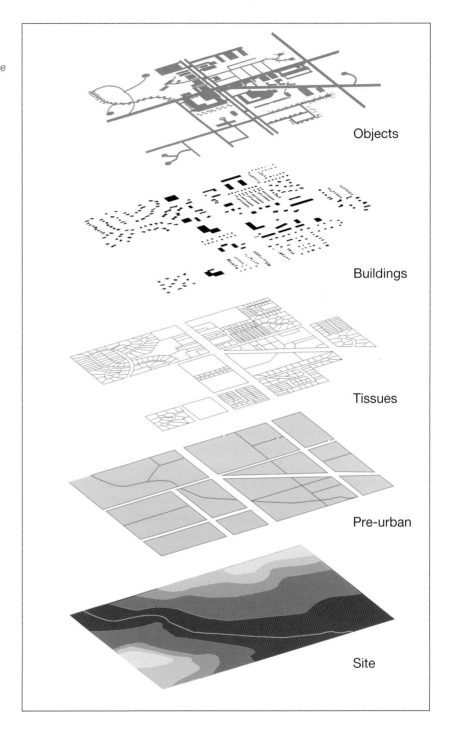

Objects

Buildings

Tissues

Pre-urban

Site

revelation in this regard, especially in the understanding of things that change easily, the fertile conditions that enable change, and changes that are more unlikely. Within existing patterns, projections of typological transformation can inform the incremental decisions and policies that drive large changes and allow the physical city to be infinitely responsive. This requires close professional observation and analysis—connoisseurship—and a keen sense of narrative.

Of particular interest is the identification of underlying patterns, especially in types, land ownership, travel, jurisdictions, and local economic and social conditions, in order to identify the history of the current development and why the place is the way it is today. Because types are the most direct and observable indication of the current and historic forces that have shaped a place, they provide strong evidence and testimony to these forces, especially if patterns are studied over time. It is easy to assume standard explanations for the decline of places—for example, "The local stores suffered when the new mall was built"—but these are more often wrong than not. Such explanations should be tested and reframed based on the physical evidence. It could be that the local stores had always suffered rapid turnover because there was too much retail space in the market. This would suggest a different strategy.

Approaching a problem from a projective perspective allows a range of possible ideas to be explored. In a single-family type neighborhood, some extremely common transformations are found over a long span of time. Examples include converting a house to a multifamily apartment building; converting a house to a business use, which requires other physical changes; and subdividing lots for infill. Teardowns, the current bad boy of urbanism, are historically very common and a reasonable way to slowly remake an obsolete neighborhood without ravaging its social character and physical plan. Social, economic, and technological changes have subtle, rather than large-scale, results in these environments because the static form and the type are both relatively stable. Taking one example of a social change, imagine what might happen if an outlying neighborhood consisted of affiliated adults, rather than a family with children, sharing a single-family type. My guess is that very little would change physically since these types have already demonstrated a strong resilience.

Other types are traditionally far more malleable. In parts of Los Angeles, John Kaliski has identified the recent evolution of a new type for auto-oriented retail, the "mini-mall," arising primarily because of much higher land costs (fig. 8-2).[6] This type is a small two-story shopping center with some of its parking underground. It supplants the less-efficient strip shopping center, on the same kind of lot. Although it is far from an ideal urban design, it has been rapidly adopted. Using this type as a jumping-off point, projective urbanism would recognize the specific conditions that form it, and work to integrate these and the type itself into a larger picture of change.

In transportation, it is easy to imagine entire roads given over to bikes instead of cars, with a network of commuter-oriented bike trails put in place. Imagine the conditions that would lead to this outcome: much higher fuel prices, dramatic improvements in bike technology, or increases of population density to the point where congestion was untenable. This infrastructural change has a much greater likelihood of altering the urban form, especially in influencing new neighborhoods and communities that are being built.

8-2 | *John Kaliski has described this emerging type in Los Angeles, the minimall, an artorial type with two stories of retail and some underground parking.*

In this book, I have avoided embracing or endorsing any one definition of "good urban design." The definition of positive change in a city necessarily shifts over time and in different places as different conditions give rise to different pathologies. In 20th-century urbanism, where the pathologies have arisen like zombies from the graveyard, this has been definitively demonstrated. It seems that just as one problem is solved—for example, traffic congestion—with Herculean effort and at great expense, the solution—limited-access highways—creates another even worse problem.

Imagination is the key. As Rem Koolhaas has written, "Since it is out of control, the urban is about to become the major vector of the imagination. Redefined, urbanism will not only, or mostly, be a profession, but a way of thinking, an ideology: to accept what exists."[7] Koolhaas goes on to suggest that, since it is all out of control, we are free to go wild, to imagine many possible cities, many possible futures.

But these future imaginings are not as unconstrained as he suggests. What *is*, what exists, constrains what is possible. Even our imaginative projections themselves, and the self-knowledge that they make clear, alter our perceptions of what may be done. Perhaps this is the most important role for urban design—not so much to tear the old down and build anew but to offer a different view of the future based on what is already happening, to develop alternative scenarios that are both plausible and exciting, to incite change through imagination.

ENDNOTES

1   Rem Koolhaas, "Whatever Happened to Urbanism?" in R. Koolhaas, B. Mau, and H. Werlemann, *S M L XL* (New York: Monacelli Press, 1995): 959–71.

2   Arthur C. Nelson, "The New Urbanity: The Rise of a New America," *The Annals of the American Academy of Political and Social Science* 626, no. 1 (2009): 192. This study projects that a 2030 surplus of single-family homes has already been constructed, based on current demographic trends.

3   Brenda Scheer, "Tipping the Sacred Cows of Planning: Whither Goes the Single-family House?" *Planning*, May 2009: 25.

4   These concepts are not new. They are harvested from ideas in the landscape urbanism movement and in other reactions to "big architecture." I am terming them projective based on a similar and closely related idea in architecture: See Robert Somol and Sarah Whiting, "Notes Around the Doppler Effect and Other Moods of Modernism," in *Perspecta: The Yale Architectural Journal* 33 (2002): 72–77.

5   Brenda Scheer, "The Anatomy of Sprawl," *Places: A Forum of Environmental Design* 14, no. 2 (Fall 2001): 25–37.

6   John Kaliski, "Minicity IV. Defining Minicity: The Architecture of Convenience," *The Architectural Correspondent*, http://thearchitecturalcorrespondent.blogspot.com/2008/11/defining-minicity-architecture-and.html.

7   Koolhaas, "Whatever Happened to Urbanism?" 971.

GRAPHICS CREDITS

All drawings, diagrams, and photos by Brenda Case Scheer, except as noted:

1-1	Photo by Newyork10R
1-2	Photo by JBC3
1-5	Drawing by Ledoux, 1804
1-6	Drawing by Paul Lukez. Used by permission. All rights reserved
1-7*,7-12*	Photo by Infrogmation of New Orleans

2-1	Engraving by Charles Eisen, 1755
2-2, 2-3, 2-4, 2-5	Rare Books Division, Special Collections, J. Willard Marriott Library, University of Utah. Used by permission
2-6	Drawings by Gianfranco Caniggia and Gian Luigi Maffei, from *Interpreting Basic Building* (Florence: Alinea Editrice, 2001)
2-7	Drawings by Rob Krier, from *Elements of Architecture*, Architectural Design Profile 49 (London: AD Publications, 1983)

3-1*	Photo by Marku1988
3-8	Drawing from James E. Packer, *The Insulae of Imperial Ostia* (Rome: American Academy in Rome, 1971)
3-9	Library of Congress, LC-DIG-ppmsc-08836
3-10	Photo by Leon H. Abdalian, 1930, Boston Public Library
3-12	Photo by Lewis Toby. Used by permission. All rights reserved
3-15	Photo by Marc Golub. Used by permission. All rights reserved
3-16*	Photo by Terence Ong
3-17*	Photo by Mark Scott Johnson
3-20	Photo by Gerard Tully. Used by permission. All rights reserved
3-24*	Photo by Sgt Fun
3-27*	Photo by White Pelican
3-28*	Photo by Ivo Shandor
3-29*	Photo by Bobak H'eri

4-3	Map of Cincinnati, published by *Drake's Natural and Statistical View*, 1815
4-5*	Photo by David Shankbone

5-1   Illustrated map published in 1817 by William Rollinson, New York Public Library Digital Gallery

6-5   Photo by David Scheer. Used by permission. All rights reserved

6-8   Illustrations by Urban Advantage. Used by permission. All rights reserved

7-14*   Photo by AgnosticPreachersKid

7-15   Library of Congress, Historic American Building Survey

8-2*   Photo by Downtowngal

*Licensed under Creative Commons by Share-Alike 3.0, see http://creativecomments.org/licenses/by-sa/3.0

BIBLIOGRAPHY

Anderson, Stanford. "Savannah and the Issue of Precedent: City Plan as Resource." *In Settlements in the Americas: Cross-cultural Perspectives*, Ralph Bennett, 114–37. Cranbury, N.J.: Associated University Press, 1993.

———. "Types and Conventions in Time: Toward a History for the Duration and Change of Artifacts." *Perspecta: Journal of the Yale School of Architecture* 18 (1982): 109–18.

Argan, Giulio Carlo. "On the Typology of Architecture." *Architectural Design* 33, no. 12 (1963): 564–65.

Baek, Kitaro. "Nishida's Philosophy of Emptiness and its Architectural Significance." *Journal of Architecture Education* 62, no. 2 (November 2008): 37–44.

Braham, William. "After Typology: The Suffering of Diagrams." *Architectural Design* 70, no. 3 (2000): 9–11.

Caniggia, Gianfranco, and Gian Luigi Maffei. *Interpreting Basic Building: Architectural Composition and Building Typology* [1979], trans. Susan Jane Fraser. Florence: Alinea Editrice, 2001.

Colquhoun, Alan. "Typology and Design Method." In *Meaning in Architecture*, ed. C. Jencks and G. Baird, 267–77. New York: George Braziller, 1969.

Conzen, M. R. G. "Alnwick, Northumberland: A Study in Town-plan Analysis." Publication No. 27. London: Institute of British Geographers, 1960.

———. "The Use of Town-plans in the Study of History." In *The Study of Urban History*, ed. H. J. Dyos, 114–30. New York: St. Martin's Press, 1968.

Davis, Howard. "The Commercial-residential Building and Local Urban Form." *Urban Morphology* 13, no. 2 (2009): 89–104.

Doern, Daniel, and Brenda Lightner. *A Pattern Book of Boston Houses*. Boston: City of Boston, 1988.

Dunham-Jones, E., and J. Williams. *Retrofitting Suburbia*. Hoboken, N.J.: John Wiley and Sons, 2009.

Durand, Jean-Nicolas-Louis. *Précis of the Lectures on Architecture; With Graphic Portion of the Lectures on Architecture* [1802], trans. David Britt. Los Angeles: Getty Research Institute, 2000.

———. *Recueil et parallèle des edifices de tout genre anciens et moderns, remarquables par leur beaute, parleur grandeur ou par leur singularite, et dessines sur une meme echelle*. Paris: Gillé, 1799.

Firley, Eric, and Caroline Stahl. *The Urban Housing Handbook: Shaping the Fabric of Our Cities*. London: John Wiley and Sons, 2009.

Goode, Terence. "Typological Theory in the U.S.: The Consumption of Architectural Authenticity." *Journal of Architectural Education* 46, no. 1 (1992): 2–13.

Habraken, N. J. *Palladio's Children: Essays on Everyday Environment and the Architect*. Oxford: Taylor and Francis, 2005.

Hall, Peter. *Cities of Tomorrow*. Oxford: Blackwell, 1988.

Hull, Steven. *Alphabet City*. New York: Pamphlet Architecture, 1982.

Jakle, John A., and Keith A. Sculle. *The Gas Station in America*. Baltimore: Johns Hopkins University Press, 1994.

Kaliski, John. "Minicity IV. Defining Minicity: The Architecture of Convenience." The Architectural Correspondent, http://thearchitecturalcorrespondent.blogspot.com/2008/11/defining-minicity-architecture-and.html, 2008.

Kelbaugh, Douglas. *Repairing the American Metropolis*. Seattle: University of Washington Press, 2002.

———. "Typology—An Architecture of Limits." *Architectural Theory Review* 1, no. 2 (November 1996): 33–52.

Koolhaas, Rem. "Whatever Happened to Urbanism?" In R. Koolhaas, B. Mau, and H. Werlemann, *S M L XL*. New York: Monacelli Press, 1995.

Krier, Léon, and Diru Thadani. *The Architecture of Community*. Washington, D.C.: Island Press, 2009.

Krier, Rob. *Elements of Architecture*. Architectural Design Profile 49. London: AD Publications, 1983.

———. *Urban Space*. New York: Rizzoli, 1979.

Lavin, Sylvia. *Quatremère de Quincy and the Invention of a Language of Modern Architecture*. Cambridge, Mass.: MIT Press, 1992.

Lukez, Paul. *Suburban Transformations*. New York: Princeton Architectural Press, 2007.

Markus, Thomas A. *Buildings and Power: Freedom and Control in the Origin of Modern Building Types*. London: Routledge, 1993.

Marzot, Nicola. "The Study of Urban Form in Italy." *Urban Morphology* 6, no. 2 (2002): 59–73.

Moneo, Raphael. "On Typology." *Oppositions* 13 (Summer 1978): 23–45.

Moudon, Anne Vernez. *Built for Change: Neighborhood Architecture in San Francisco*. Cambridge, Mass.: MIT Press, 1986.

———. "A Catholic Approach to Organizing What Urban Designers Should Know." *Journal of Planning Literature* 6 (May 1992): 332–49.

———. "Getting to Know the Built Landscape: Typomorphology." In *Ordering Space: Type in Architecture and Design*, ed. Karen A. Franck and Linda Schneekloth, 289–308. New York: Van Nostrand Reinhold, 1994.

Nelson, Arthur C. "The New Urbanity: The Rise of a New America." *The Annals of the American Academy of Political and Social Science* 626, no. 1 (2009): 192.

Nesbitt, Kate. *Theorizing a New Agenda for Architecture: An Anthology of Architectural Theory 1965–1995*. New York: Princeton Architectural Press, 1996.

Packer, James E. *The Insulae of Imperial Ostia*. Rome: American Academy in Rome, 1971.

Parolek, D., K. Parolek, and P. Crawford. *Form-Based Codes*. Hoboken, N.J.: John Wiley and Sons, 2008.

Petruccioli, Attilio. "Exoteric—Polytheistic—Fundamentalist Typology: Gleanings in the Form of an Introduction." In *Typological Process and Design Theory*, 9–17. Cambridge, Mass.: Aga Khan Program for Islamic Architecture, 1998.

Pevsner, Sir Nikolaus. *A History of Building Types*. London: Thames and Hudson, 1976.

Picon, Antoine. "From 'Poetry of Art' to Method: The Theory of Jean-Nicholas-Louis Durand." In J. N. L. Durand, *Précis of the Lectures on Architecture; With Graphic Portion of the Lectures on Architecture* [1802], trans. David Britt. Los Angeles: Getty Research Institute, 2000.

Porphyrios, Demetri. "Leon Krier – Houses, Palaces, Cities." *Architectural Design* 7/8 (1984): 2–128.

Quatremère de Quincy, A. C. "Type." Introd. Anthony Vidler. *Oppositions* 8 (Spring 1977): 147–50.

Rossi, Aldo. *Architecture of the City* [1966], trans. Diane Ghirardo and Joan Ockman. Cambridge, Mass.: MIT Press. Oppositions Books, 1982.

Rowe, Peter. *Design Thinking*. Cambridge, Mass.: MIT Press, 1987.

Rybczynski, Witold. "Architects Must Listen to the Melody." *New York Times*. September 24, 1989.

Scheer, Brenda. "The Anatomy of Sprawl." *Places: A Forum of Environmental Design* 14, no. 2 (Fall 2001): 25–37.

———. "Invitation to Debate." In *Design Review: Challenging Aesthetic Control*, ed. Brenda Case Scheer and Wolfgang F. E. Preiser, 1–10. New York: Chapman and Hall, 1994.

———. "The Radial Street as a Timeline: A Study of the Transformation of Elastic Tissues." In *Suburban Form, an International Perspective*, ed. Kiril Stanilov and Brenda Scheer, 102–22. London: Routledge, 2003.

———. "Tipping the Sacred Cows of Planning: Whither Goes the Single-family House?" *Planning*, May 2009:25.

———. "Who Made This Big Mess?" *Urban Design*, no. 93 (Winter 2005): 25–27.

Scheer, Brenda, and Daniel Ferdelman. "Destruction and Survival: The Story of Over-the-Rhine." *Urban Morphology* 5, no. 2 (2001): 15–27.

Scheer, Brenda, and Mintcho Petkov. "Edge City Morphology: A Comparison of Commercial Centers." *Journal of the American Planning Association* 64, no. 3 (Summer 1998): 298–310.

Schon, Donald A. "Designing: Rules, Types, Worlds." *Design Studies* 9, no. 3 (July 1988): 181–90.

Southworth, Michael, and Peter Owens. "The Evolving Metropolis: Studies of Community, Neighborhood, and Street Form at the Urban Edge." *Journal of the American Planning Association* 59, no. 3 (Summer 1993): 271–87.

Storey, Glen. "The Meaning of Insula in Roman Residential Terminology." *Memoirs of the American Academy in Rome*. Vol. 49:47–84. Ann Arbor, Mich.: University of Michigan Press for the American Academy in Rome, 2004.

Tze Ling Li. "A Study of the Facades of Colonial Shophouses in Singapore." *Journal of Asian Architecture and Building Engineering* 6, no. 1 (May 2007): 42–48.

Vanderburgh, David. "Typology." In *Encyclopedia of 20th-Century Architecture*, vol. 3. Ed. R. Stephen Sennott. London: Fitzroy Dearborn, 2003.

Vidler, Anthony. "The Idea of Type: The Transformation of the Academic Ideal, 1750–1830." *Oppositions* 8 (Spring 1977): 93–113.

———. "The Third Typology." *Oppositions* 7 (Winter 1976): 3–4.

———. *The Writing of the Walls: Architectural Theory in the Late Enlightenment*. Princeton, N.J.: Princeton Architectural Press, 1987.

Villari, Sergio. *J. N. L. Durand (1760–1834): Art and Science of Architecture*. New York: Rizzoli International, 1990.

Whaley, Lindsay J. *Introduction to Typology: The Unity and Diversity of Language*. Thousand Oaks, Calif.: Sage, 1997.

Wheeler, Stephen M. "Built Landscapes in Metropolitan Regions." *Journal of Planning Education and Research* 27 (2008): 400–416.

INDEX

About the Author

Brenda Case Scheer, AICP, has been dean of the College of Architecture and Planning at the University of Utah for eight years. She is a registered architect and certified planner. She received architecture degrees from Rice University and was a Loeb Fellow at the Harvard Graduate School of Design.

Scheer is a noted scholar, with 19 research grants or contracts, and 24 book chapters and journal articles. Most of her work is used to inform designers and policy makers who combat sprawl and protect significant places. While teaching and writing, she has continued to practice architecture with the award-winning firm of Scheer & Scheer.

Scheer sits on multiple professional and community boards, including the Landscape Architecture Foundation, the GSA Peer Reviewers, the National Endowment for the Arts Mayors' Institute on City Design, the Envision Utah executive committee, and the board of Artspace, in Salt Lake City. She was an instrumental adviser to the Salt Lake Chamber of Commerce during its massive and far-reaching Downtown Rising Project. She is appointed by the mayor of Salt Lake to the city's Redevelopment Advisory Committee and is also appointed to the board of the county's Center for the Arts, which oversees cultural facilities. She is a site visitor for both the Planning Accreditation Board and the National Architect Accreditation Board. She has served on the editorial board of several journals including the *Journal of the American Planning Association*.